D0323608

HOW
JESUS
HELPED PEOPLE

HOW
JESUS
HELPED PEOPLE

Alan Walker

ABINGDON PRESS New York—Nashville

HOW JESUS HELPED PEOPLE

Dedicated to

all who staff

the Sydney Life Line Center

where help is as close as the telephone

CONTENTS

How Jesus Helped People

JESUS
AND A LONELY MAN

If Jesus came walking among us today I could imagine him saying, "Come unto me all you who are lonely and I will give you friendship." Loneliness has become a great modern sickness of the soul. It is a far more serious malaise than we realize. It is at its worst in the cities of the world, where people are lost in the lonely crowd. In rural areas everybody knows everybody. In cities we scarcely know the name of the next-door-but-one neighbor or the family in the

9

apartment above. If Jesus of Nazareth is to help many of us today, he must offer us an answer to loneliness.

There is a story in the Bible about how Jesus brought friendship to a rejected, lonely man named Zacchaeus. Zacchaeus lived in Jericho when Jericho was an important trading city, situated astride the caravan routes of the ancient world.

Zacchaeus was the chief tax gatherer of Jericho. This meant he was a collaborator with the Roman Empire. The Romans sold tax gathering rights to the highest bidder. The tax gatherer then exacted all he could from the people to cover cost and make profit.

Tax gatherers became a hated class. They were looked upon as both exploiters and traitors. No Jew loyal to the traditions of his people had any friendly dealings with a tax gatherer. Children spat on the ground as a tax gatherer walked by, reflecting popular rejection and disgust. Of all people he was a lonely man.

When Jesus came to Jericho Zacchaeus was eager to see him. Perhaps he had heard stories of the respect and friendship Jesus offered to outcasts. At least Zacchaeus was so determined to catch a glimpse of Jesus that he, a small man, climbed a tree the better to see him pass by.

To his utter surprise Jesus stopped beneath him. "Zacchaeus, make haste and come down," he said. Unbelieving, the little man obeyed. Before the amazed, resentful stares of the crowd he and Jesus set out together toward his home.

10

Before the night was over the friendship of Jesus had transformed Zacchaeus' life. "The half of my goods I give to the poor; and if I have defrauded any one of anything, I restore it fourfold." Friendship, the friendship of Jesus, had worked its miracle. "Salvation," said Jesus, "has come to this house."

The most startling fact in the story of Jesus and Zacchaeus is that Jesus stopped and spoke to the lonely outcast. We can almost hear the gasp of surprise as we read of what happened. Neither Zacchaeus nor the crowd hid their astonishment that Jesus took the initiative, offering his friendship to the man who was up the Jericho tree.

Lonely people usually remain in their loneliness until someone cares enough to get through to them. It is the nature of loneliness to turn us in on ourselves. We become like people in prison, we cannot escape. Our very aloneness makes us unpleasant and unattractive, which separates us further from those about us.

Here in Sydney, after four years of planning, we have established what is called the Life Line Center. At its heart is the telephone. Twenty-four hours a day the telephone is staffed by mature Christian volunteers who have been trained over many months to offer friendship and counsel to all who may call. Life Line has as its simple slogan: Help is as close as the telephone.

Life Line offers what may be called "answers in depth." Hence, behind the telephone is a series of specialized people and agencies. At the center there is a full-time staff of Christian ministers, marriage counselors, psychiatrists, a nursing sister, and social workers. All are available for follow-up service for those who turn to the center for aid.

Many an emergency call reaches Life Line. Such come especially from would-be suicide cases, for it is in part a suicide-prevention center. Then the "trouble team" may go into action. Always there is on call a team of two people who can rush in the radio-controlled cars of the center to the place and situation of need.

Life Line could not operate without the disciplined strength which the Life Line Movement gives it. This is a lay movement which all who wish to serve through the Life Line Center must join. It has five divisions: telephone counselors, caring division, area visitors, young Life Liners, and general service. Members must accept a fivefold pledge, the first of which is to accept Jesus Christ as Savior and Lord. Training courses and a probation period are required of all who are finally accepted as members.

Life Line has grown out of the needs of a vast city. It is a strange experience to sit at the nerve center in the $140,000 building which has been erected for Life Line. The nerve center is the main telephone counseling room. There, at all hours of the day and night, counselors sit just waiting for the telephone to ring. And ring it does. In the first year of operation over twelve thousand people dialed the Life Line number.

The calls which come to Life Line cover the whole gamut of human need. However, we are amazed how often there is an ingredient of loneliness in the situation with which we grapple. People, isolated, anxious distraught, often ring just to talk to someone. If there is anything Life Line is proving it is that there is a terrible loneliness which lies behind the face of a city and lurks within the depths of a mass society.

We are discovering how vulnerable to temptation loneliness makes people. Alcoholism, compulsive gambling, sexual abnormalities, even crime, result from loneliness.

Leslie Weatherhead tells of this fact in a conversation he had with a girl who spoke to him on a London street. He found she had come from the country to the city, and gradually was drawn into a life of impurity. Her explanation was simply, "I was lonely, I lost the fight."

Yet we should need no proof of the seriousness of loneliness. A lonely man is half a man. Sartre says: "Without a looker-on a man evaporates." The Bible puts it this way: "It is not good for man to be alone" (Gen. 2:16, Moffatt).

Jesus knew the meaning of loneliness. Perhaps that is why he sensed the need of the outcast of Jericho. Once the crowds thronged around Jesus, but presently they dwindled away until he said to the few remaining: "Will you also go away?" His own family gave him little understanding, and he knew the acute suffering of seeing the puzzlement, even the condemnation, on the faces of those dearest to him. At last the disciples failed him. "They all forsook him and fled." In the end he stood alone, absolutely alone.

Jesus took the initiative with Zacchaeus, offering friendship. He takes the initiative with us. No life longs for the companionship of Christ without his knowing it. At once he is there, offering friendship to the lonely. Jesus said to Zacchaeus, "Make haste and come down; for I must stay at your house today."

There is a scene in Lloyd Douglas' story "The Mirror" in which he imagines a conversation between Jesus and Zacchaeus. "Zacchaeus," said Jesus gently: "What did you see that made you desire this peace?" "Good Master," was the reply, "I saw, mirrored in your eyes, the face of the Zacchaeus I was meant to be."

The story of Zacchaeus is a wonderful example of the way Jesus helped people by restoring to them dignity and self-respect. As we watch Jesus and Zacchaeus setting off together down the street, the little man Zacchaeus seems inches taller and his shoulders are square and his head upright. He is walking with Jesus.

Only Zacchaeus would know what it meant to hear Jesus say: "He also is a son of Abraham." No one had thought of or called him by that name for years. They had many a name for Zacchaeus, ugly names, hateful names. Traitors and treason have always brought forth more hatred than most things. But Jesus changed it all. He said: "He also is a son of Abraham."

We are all deeply influenced by the image we think other people have of us. When we believe other people respect and trust us, we try to convince them and ourselves that the image is right. When others doubt and condemn us, we become careless, even in a twisted way almost finding satisfaction in living according to our reputations.

I was recently grappling with a boy who had been convicted of stealing. Gradually his story began to unfold. Some money left for a milkman on the step of his home disappeared. His father charged him with the theft, and as punishment confiscated his much loved transistor radio. The boy's response was to steal. "They think I am a thief, so I may as well be one," was his bitter comment. He proved to my satisfaction that he was innocent of the first charge against him. But his parents doubted and rejected him, so he began to live according to their image of him.

Jesus, says W. E. Sangster, "sees double." He sees us not only as we are, but as we might become by his grace. It is this confidence in us which holds us and leads us on. Jesus at Jericho saw Zacchaeus not only as he was, a collaborator with Rome, but as he yearned to be, a Jew proud of his race. "You are a son of Abraham." And that is what he began again to be, when Jesus put his trust in him.

A legend comes down to us of Zacchaeus as an old man. Zacchaeus still lived in his house by the Jericho road. Often he could be seen walking slowly to a tree not far from his home. He would spend time in its shade. Sometimes he would almost caressingly rest his hand on its trunk and branches.

"Why do you care for this old sycamore tree?" he was asked. "Because from the boughs of this old tree I first saw my Lord," was his quiet reply.

Friendship with Jesus opens the way to a new relationship with others. Friends of Jesus become friends with one another.

Bible stories are so brief they always leave a great deal to the imagination. There are several gaps in the story of Zacchaeus. The account jumps from the two men setting off for the home of Zacchaeus to the bold declaration of the tax gatherer: "The half of my goods I give to the poor; and if I have defrauded any one of anything, I restore it fourfold."

Jesus must have spoken frankly to Zacchaeus. He perhaps urged him to take such steps as he could to put right his relationships with others.

I wonder what it is that lies behind some of our alienation from others, behind our loneliness. Do we need to write a letter to someone asking forgiveness? Do we need to show a new compassion, a new generosity, to those about us? We cannot buy friendship, but some action on our part will clear away obstructions and allow friendship to flow.

No one will ever be able to calculate what people

lose by failing to become linked with the amazing fellowship to be found in the Christian church. Becoming a member of the Christian church, the greatest society on earth, brings many blessings. It links people together on the deepest of all levels, the level of the spirit. It is the broadest fellowship to be found, for the universal company of Christians stretches to the end of the earth.

Jesus gave us the church to be a small company of people set down in every community. In that fellowship we become aware that we count not only to God but in the sight of one another. Around the mutual friend Jesus, mutual friends gather.

There is a simple, popular hymn which Christians often sing together in our churches. The simple fact is that it is true.

> Blest be the tie that binds
> Our hearts in Christian love:
>
> .   .   .   .
>
> We share each other's woes,
> Each other's burdens bear,
> And often for each other flows
> The sympathizing tear.

To become a friend of Jesus is to become a friend of God. When Jesus comes into our hearts and our homes, the worst alienation of all is ended, alienation from God.

The climax of the Zacchaeus story is when Jesus said to him: "Today salvation has come to this house, for

17

the Son of Man came to seek and to save the lost."
The lonely heart of Zacchaeus was suddenly flooded
with the love of God.

There is no loneliness to equal the loneliness of sin.
Sin possesses the strange power of making us feel
separated from life itself. It makes us feel as though
we are orphans in a vast universe.

"Religion," says Alfred North Whitehead, "is what
a man does with his solitariness." It is true. The es-
sence of religion is companionship with God. The
Bible often speaks of this companionship: "I will never
... forsake thee." Jesus, as always, speaks for God when
his promise is given: "Lo, I am with you always, to the
close of the age."

At every stage of our life the friendship of Christ,
the companionship of God, can be ours. A child can
sing:

> Jesus loves me, this I know,
> For the Bible tells me so.

In the teenage years when young people yearn so
desperately for friendship, Christ allows us to sing:
"Just a closer walk with Thee." The mid-years bring
the harshness of life's struggle, but they also carry
the assurance that Zacchaeus found: "I must stay at
your house today."

Martin Luther starkly describes the loneliness at the
end of the road. "Every man must fight his own battle

with death. In that hour I may not stand with you or you with me." But Someone does remain with us: "Thy rod and thy staff they comfort me."

Just a lonely man? No, lonely no longer. And Jesus said to Zacchaeus, and says again to you and me: "Make haste, and come down; for I must stay at your house today."

JESUS
AND A DIVORCEE

When I was in Palestine, there
was one place where I knew for certain I was standing
where Jesus had stood. It was at Jacob's well, one of
the best-authenticated sites in the world. I approached
the well from the modern town of Nablus. The well is
in a compound with a path running to it across the
dusty earth. As is usual in Palestine, the sacred spot
is somewhat spoiled by man's attempt to embellish it.
In this case a Greek Orthodox church is built above it.

20

Here the building does not seem even to be completed.

No one has been able to mar the well itself. It was dug by Jacob about seventeen hundred years before Jesus. It must have been a deep well for even today, after stones and rubble have fallen in, it goes down to a depth of seventy-five feet. It is a yard wide at the top, perhaps three times that width lower down. In it there still springs up clear, soft, fresh water.

There was a woman there, and she lowered a cup to the level of the water and I took it and drank. The moment was as sacred as any of Holy Communion, for Christ was very near. I was deeply moved as I seemed to hear his words spoken long ago: "Whoever drinks of the water that I shall give him shall never thirst; the water that I shall give him will become in him a spring of water welling up to eternal life."

It was at Jacob's well that there took place one of the most thrilling encounters in all history. It was between Jesus and a divorcee from the nearby town of Sychar.

Jesus was on his way from Judea to Galilee. He came, dusty and tired, at noon to the well. He sent his disciples to Sychar for food, while he remained at the well. Presently a woman appeared, walking gracefully with a waterpot balanced on her head.

"Give me a drink," said Jesus. The woman was startled in a way difficult for us to grasp. First of all, she was a Samaritan, and the quarrel between Jews and Samaritans was so bitter that normally neither spoke to the other. Then, too, she was a woman, and Jewish social custom decreed that out of doors a man did not speak to a woman.

From this simple beginning developed one of the most exciting conversations recorded in the Bible. The intellectual level of the discussion leaves us rather breathless. "How is it that you, a Jew, ask a drink of me, a woman of Samaria?" Then they are into it. Jesus says that if she knew who he was she would be asking a drink of him. Flippantly she answers: "You have nothing to draw with, and the well is deep."

There is nothing casual or light in the exchanges that follow. Soon the woman finds her life laid bare. Jesus reminds her she has been five times married, and that the one with whom she is then living is only a *de facto* husband.

Again reality breaks through. Somehow the differences in the worship of God between Jews and Samaritans get into the discussion. Quietly Jesus says: "God is spirit, and those who worship him must worship in spirit and truth."

The sudden hush between them is disturbed by the returning disciples. Embarrassed, the woman hurries away to tell the people of Sychar: "Come, see a man who told me all that I ever did." Out hurry the Samaritans, and Jesus is encouraged to stay for two days in the village, many coming to believe "this is indeed the Savior of the world."

Jesus made his first contact with the divorcee at the

well by a simple device. He asked her for help. "Give me a drink," he said.

Nothing puts people so quickly at ease as to be asked for help. By asking, we place ourselves at the mercy of another, accepting a lower, inferior position to the other. Confidence is thus born, and a relationship is opened up.

During his lifetime Jesus often asked help of people. He borrowed a boat to speak to the people on the shores of Galilee. He won entrance into the heart of Zacchaeus by asking if he could stay the night under his roof. How excited the boy must have been when Jesus asked if he could have his picnic lunch of bread and fish to feed the hungry crowd. Jesus sent his disciples to a friend to ask if he could have the use of a donkey to ride into Jerusalem.

"Give me a drink." These are still the words Jesus speaks to us, placing us at our ease. He is reaching out to us when any thirsty child asks for a cup of water. His pleading eyes are reflected in every hungry man or woman in overcrowded lands. His need is seen in the lonely, distressed, and distraught who haunt the great cities of a mass society. His yearning for communion with God throbs in the life of all who have lost him or have not yet heard of him.

How do we know? Why he told us. "I was hungry and you gave me food, I was thirsty and you gave me a drink. . . . I was sick and you visited me, I was in prison and you came to me."

But he is not in need today. Yes, he is, for he said: "As you did it to one of the least of these my brethren, you did it to me."

"Give me a drink" The cry of Christ comes from all the world. As Douglas Houton told the New Delhi Assembly of the World Council of Churches, "I was a hungry child in that village near Calcutta and you gave me meat. I was a thirsty native in the outback of Australia and you gave me drink. I was a stranger on the New York streets and you took me in, naked in Ecuador and you clothed me. I was sick in Düsseldorf and you visited me. I was in prison in Angola and you came to me."

With contact made, Jesus is soon at grips with the deepest life of the woman at the well. There is strength and sympathy in his voice as he uncovers her rather seamy marital life and speaks to her about it.

Divorce is no modern problem. Moses had to legislate regarding it centuries before Jesus. Jesus confronted it as a moral issue. "You have had five husbands and he whom you now have is not your husband." No, it is not modern Hollywood but ancient Sychar.

What was the attitude of Jesus to divorce? On one occasion the Pharisees forced him to face the issue as bluntly as he could. "Is it lawful for a man to divorce his wife?" they asked.

The New Testament unfortunately seems to give two different answers from Jesus: One in Mark and one in Matthew. Some interpret Mark as meaning that

Jesus made no provision for divorce under any circumstances. Others, quoting Matthew, declare Jesus made one exception. He permitted divorce for "unchastity."

To build a case for Christ's attitude toward divorce in either Mark or Matthew seems to me to be wrong. Jesus repudiated legalistic answers to all questions. And he did it about divorce. He lifts the whole issue into the realm of great moral and spiritual—and human —principles.

What, then, does Jesus establish? He declares that the marriage of one man and one woman for life is God's plan and purpose. To him marriage is implied in the creation of male and female. He says bluntly: "What therefore God has joined together let no man put asunder."

Jesus, ever a champion of womanhood, places men and women on an absolutely equal level in marriage and in any procedures related to possible divorce. In Hebrew society, which gave privilege and precedence to men, Jesus declared the equal rights of women. Husbands and wives are to be treated alike.

A reading of all Jesus says about divorce seems to indicate that he accepted the law of Moses which with great limitations permitted divorce. He recognized that the sin of man must be taken into account. Jesus pointed out that divorce was permitted in the book of Deuteronomy for "hardness of heart." He too appears to recognize that human sin makes divorce in some cases almost inevitable.

25

There is one fact which stands out starkly in the conversation with the much-married woman at the well. There is sympathy and understanding of the unhappiness of her life. There is an acceptance of her life, stained and soiled as it is. Above all, divorce does not debar her from receiving the gift of eternal life which he offers. He accepts her as she is, and seeks to lead her on to the new beginning which his grace makes possible to all who are willing to receive it.

Jesus always took people as he found them. None was debarred from the chance of starting again. None was excluded from the love and salvation he offered. In the light of his understanding, firmness, and sympathy, how do modern church attitudes appear? I find no endorsement of the "hard line" adopted toward divorce and remarriage by certain of the great churches of the world. Somehow I think Jesus, while doing nothing to weaken the sanctity of marriage, would still offer the ministries of his grace in the marriage service and Holy Communion to those who "for hardness of heart" had failed and sinned. However soiled and stained we may be, to us he comes offering his all.

After all, it was to a divorcee that Jesus said, "Whoever drinks of the water that I shall give him will never thirst." And there was no rejection of that sudden earnest cry of a life to whom hope had suddenly come: "Give me this water that I may not thirst."

Jesus made a tremendous claim to the Samaritan woman by Jacob's well. He declared that he could give permanent satisfaction to the parched human spirit.

I wonder why divorce is so common? I wonder why there have always been women, ancient and modern, who go from husband to husband? To face the sheer unhappiness and distress of one divorce must be torture indeed, but to go through it again and again must represent misery unlimited.

There is one possible explanation. It can be seen so clearly in the stories of the unhappy film stars of Hollywood. Some people go from man to man and woman to woman in the hope somewhere of finding happiness. Inner satisfaction is falsely sought in a frantic changing of marriage partners.

It was to a five-times-married divorcee that Jesus said, "Whoever drinks of the water I shall give him will never thirst." Here alone at last, he was saying, is the answer to the search that had driven her so far.

The simple truth is that there is something in human nature which only God can satisfy. Made in the image of God the human spirit cries out for God. There is no substitute for him. "Deep calls to deep," says the Bible. Only God can fill the "God-shaped blank" in many a heart.

A million witnesses could confirm Jesus' claim to be able to quench man's eternal thirst. As Jesus said, the water he gives is as a spring welling up constantly.

The water Jesus offers is never exhausted. Never can his resources be drained dry. The water Jesus gives never grows stale. His truth remains fresh, satisfying always. The life of God offered us in Jesus never satiates. The more of his grace we receive, the more we want.

Let one testimony stand for many. Joseph Rank, the wealthy flour miller of England, had power and riches and widespread public acclaim. Yet wherein lay his deepest satisfaction? To a questioner he spoke of the service he gave in Christ's name as a Methodist Sunday-school teacher. Quietly he said: "Nothing gives me more consolation than my work in the Sunday school."

It is just true. Whoever drinks of the water Jesus gives him will never, never thirst. It is as a "spring of water welling up to eternal life."

So we can sing Harry Loes' hymn:

> He satisfies me so
> His constant peace I know
> My all I'll give for Him to live
> He satisfies me so.

Surely no one can read how Jesus spoke with the woman by Jacob's well without sensing his gentle wisdom, his searching, probing, even relentless spirit, as he sought to help her.

The conversation between Jesus and the divorcee shows the woman seeking to evade facing the truth. As so often happens in a counseling situation, there was a running from reality. It all began so simply; just a request from a stranger for a drink. Before she realizes it she is talking of eternal things.

28

Then, suddenly, it is her own life which is in the center of conversation. "Go, call your husband." With a half-truth, which was meant to mislead, she said, "I have no husband." Then comes the devastating revelation. Jesus knows all about her, the five husbands, the divorces, the present *de facto* relationship.

This is much too revealing to be comfortable, so she tries to change the subject. She begins talking about the religious differences between the Jews and the Samaritans. She was not really interested, but it took the spotlight off herself.

There is no escape, for deeper than ever she is taken. A sudden hush falls as she hears the wonderful words: "God is spirit, and those who worship him must worship in spirit and in truth." Down that last evasive laneway she has run, only to meet God himself. For suddenly she knows she is in the presence of God, there at noonday by the well.

How we all try to evade reality! How we run from God. We too discuss and argue, our very intellectual pretensions cloaking God. We too sometimes claim it is the difference between religions or the disunity of the churches which supposedly worries us. In our hearts we know this is an excuse, an excuse to avoid looking into the face of God. We too imagine it is doubt which hides God from us, when it is really guilt.

God, in Jesus, does not allow us to escape. He loves us too much to let us go. So the loving, relentless search goes on for our souls. He pierces all our defenses, He

29

uncovers all our hiding places. In the end we stand before him, able to avoid him no longer.

The end of the incident by the well was acceptance of the claims of the Christ. Others too were brought to his side. The people in nearby Sychar said simply, "This is indeed the Savior of the world."

Stop running away from God. Cease looking for answers to life's yearnings anywhere else save in God himself. Christ waits for you and me to say, "This is indeed the Savior of the world."

JESUS
AND THE WOMAN
WITH AN INCURABLE
DISEASE

Nothing is more impressive in
the story of Jesus than the way he helped people. With
untiring compassion he went out to meet the puzzled
and the fearful, the mentally sick and physically ill,
taking healing wherever he went. To the anxious and
the sinful he gave deliverance, communicating forgiveness and peace. So much so that to read the story is
to exclaim again and again, "How Jesus helped people!"

One of the loveliest stories of Christ meeting human need is the encounter between Jesus and a woman with an incurable disease. Jesus came across the Sea of Galilee and landed near the town of Capernaum. His coming had been known, and a crowd had gathered. As he walked toward the city, an important person, a ruler of the country, stopped him and urged him desperately to hurry to his sick child's bedside. At once Jesus responded, but as he set out the crowd followed him as a great retinue.

As Jesus hurried along a narrow road of Palestine, he suddenly stopped and turning said, "Who touched me?" His disciples quickly answered, "Oh, Jesus, what a question to ask. Look at the narrow laneway and the huge crowd, and yet you ask who touched you." "No," said Jesus, "it was no accident, somebody deliberately touched me. Who was it?" No longer hidden by the crowd, a shy little woman stepped up from behind him and blurted out the story of her life. Quietly she told of twelve years of sickness and her hopes as she confessed, "I touched you, Jesus." Then she hears the wonderful words: "Daughter, your faith has made you well; go in peace."

I want you to think about this woman suffering from an incurable disease. It is a story of great significance and beauty, and it speaks directly to us all. Many of us live within the anonymous crowds of our day. Hopefully we reach out a finger to touch Jesus. We are conscious perhaps of some chronic, seemingly incurable weakness of body, mind, or spirit. So we come hoping to touch him, yearning to hear him say to us: "Your faith has made you well; go in peace."

In the story of the woman with an incurable disease we see a wonderful example of the sensitiveness of Jesus. Here he was in a crowded laneway so typical of Palestine. Even today the little passageways which run through the villages are narrow in the extreme. Along one of these lanes waited a humble woman, a person of no account socially, drawn by the news that Jesus of Nazareth was to pass by.

Jesus was on an important errand. Jairus, a ruler of the Jews, had appealed to Jesus because his child was sick. Jesus showed no special interest in very important people. It was need, just need, which always reached his heart. So a quiet, anonymous woman in a crowd suddenly found herself facing Jesus. Mark Guy Pearse puts it this way: "She began as a Nobody, she became a Somebody and she ended as Everybody."

Christ, the sensitive Christ, stopped, halted by need. One of the greatest intellectual problems we face is how the God of all the universe and of this overcrowded planet with its three billion people could be interested in us.

God is the God of the particular. A butterfly wing under a microscope is distinctive; no two wings, even of the same species, are ever the same. When the hairs of a man's or a woman's head are put under the microscope, no single hair looks exactly like any other hair.

The same is true of fingerprints. No two fingerprints have been found to be alike. God, who is the God of all the universe and the Heavenly Father of multitudes, is apparently concerned about the particular. He does not duplicate his work. He makes people separate and particular.

On a recent car trip to Melbourne, we found one evening that a sparrow had beeen caught on the radiator of the car. As I threw that little bird's body into the gutter, I thought of the words of Jesus that not a sparrow falls to the ground without God noticing it. Jesus, by his utterances, confirmed God's interest in each individual life. Hence in the story of the woman at Capernaum the crowd is forgotten. It becomes just Jesus and a woman in need. The sensitive Christ is halted by the touch of need. And the answer in love is given: "Your faith has made you well; go in peace."

Jesus gave to the woman at Capernaum the gift she asked of him, physical healing. As we think of her, we are confronted with the mystery and the power of the healing ministry of Jesus.

What a pathetic picture is given in this account of an incurable disease. This woman in the city of Capernaum, nameless, suffered from an issue of blood. She had suffered for twelve years from frequent hemorrhage. I guess every woman understands something of the distress and the burden that this would be. She had been to all the doctors, going to them one by one. She experienced what many a modern person has done with an

34

incurable disease, she had spent all she had. Even so, there was no sign of healing; perhaps she was getting worse.

There was another reason why she carried so heavy a load. In Judaism taboos surrounded a person who had an issue of blood. If you go back into the book of Leviticus you will find that the Jews had peculiar fears about anything that issued from the body of a man or a woman. They even laid down regulations for this kind of disease. Leviticus reads: "If a woman has a discharge of blood many years all the days of the discharge, she is unclean." This meant this woman could not go to worship, she could not share in the act of sacrifice. Also anybody who touched her became unclean. Hence there were special regulations about how she was to wash her clothes, even about where she was allowed to sit. Thus, there was an awful burden ritualistically placed upon this poor woman, adding to the burden of her sickness.

The New Testament presents Jesus as the great physician. Look at the facts. There are twenty-six separate healing stories in the Gospels. There are ten occasions where Jesus healed groups of people. Four times there is this type of comment: "He went about healing all manner of sickness and disease among the people."

Jesus offered salvation for the whole person, including healing of the body. In the early church healing power was expressed. There is the significant comment in the book of James: "Is any among you sick? Let him call for the elders of the church." Yet by the third century the gift of healing seems almost to be lost. Cyprian said: "The sins of Christians have weakened the power of the Church."

Today the church is groping its way back toward the faith and the power needed for a healing ministry. Science itself is opening the way. The relationship between spirit and body, mind and physical health, is being realized as never before. Now the wholeness of the approach to healing is recognized, for it is not the *body*, it is the *man* who is sick.

Jesus is able to help us in our sickness and disease; it was also for this purpose he came amongst us. To his sensitive concern is added the ability to heal. The promise of scripture is kept: "This was to fulfil what was spoken by the prophet Isaiah, 'He took our infirmities and bare our sicknesses.'"

The woman of Capernaum came to Jesus as a last resort. She had been to everybody, for the story says she had "suffered much under many physicians, and had spent all that she had, and was no better but rather grew worse." There was no offense in Jesus; he was willing to be even a last resort.

I am deeply moved when I think of the patience and the magnanimity of Jesus. So often he has to wait until we have run along many a bypath, until we have tried almost everything and everyone else. But as with the

Prodigal Son, he quietly waits until we "come to our-selves."

People turn to Christ with one of two motives. Some feel the pull of his love and the attractiveness of his person. Others are pushed by inner need and outer circumstances toward him. Whether we are pulled or pushed he receives us, such is his love for us.

Walter Russell Maltby has caught Christ's mood of being willing to receive us, broken and beaten, even when we treat him only as a last resort. He imagines a conversation between "Wonder and the Shepherd."

Wonder: Where are you going, Shepherd?
Shepherd: To find my sheep.
Wonder: How far will you go?
Shepherd: As far as my sheep.
Wonder: How far may that be?
Shepherd: To the world's end.
Wonder: How long will you seek it?
Shepherd: Until I find it.
Wonder: When you find it, will it come to you?
Shepherd: No, it will fly from me.
Wonder: Where will it go then?
Shepherd: To the rocks and the sand.
Wonder: When will it stop?
Shepherd: When it can run no more.
Wonder: What will you do then?
Shepherd: Carry it home.

Then we must notice it was a very little faith that proved sufficient for the woman with an incurable disease to be healed, just a little faith.

Jesus probably wore a cloak over his shoulders. As was the custom of the Jews, a tassel or fringe was sewed to each of the four corners of the cloak. It was perhaps one of these tassels that the woman pulled as Jesus walked by. Certainly the Greek word used in the New Testament meant "to pull at a tassel." In other words it was a deliberate act of faith on her part.

Throughout the whole story of Jesus we see glimpses of how much he can do with a little. What did Simon the fisherman know of Jesus when asked to follow him? At that stage he could have had no more than a rudimentary faith in Jesus. But it was enough to launch him on his journey to greatness.

What did the dying thief, hanging beside Jesus on the cross, know of the suffering Christ? Perhaps he had scarcely seen Jesus before. But amid the tumult of pain, some impression touched the depth of his being. Quietly he said: "Remember me when you come in your kingly power." It was only a rudimentary stirring of faith. But it was enough. He had given Christ something to build on: "Today you will be with me in Paradise."

There worshiped with us recently a woman doctor from Queensland. With joy she reminded me of her story, a story I knew well. Proudly she introduced me to her teen-age family.

What was the story? In the Australian Mission to the Nation, we broadcast on a nationwide radio network a weekly religious program called, "Drama with a Challenge." This doctor, one Tuesday night, was standing distraught in her office. In her hand was a glass of prepared poison. In her mind was a resolute determination to drink it.

Suddenly a Christian word came from the radio in the corner of the room. God used that word to arrest her mind. She began to listen. Then slowly, with a new purpose struggling in her mind, she poured the poison down a washbasin. Brokenly, dimly, she glimpsed another way of facing her troubles. Later, she told me she knelt on that office floor and surrendered her life to Christ. Months of struggle lay ahead, but through it all her faith, at first so small and fragile, strengthened. She took her place in a church, she moved out into Christian leadership. Now she says she has never really looked back from that night when with slight, groping faith she found her Lord.

Jesus no more rejects us for inadequacy of faith than he does for unworthiness of life. Sinful or doubting we may come. A little faith is sufficient. The mustard seed grows, becoming the greatest of the herbs. Jesus takes us as we are, making us what he wants us to be.

First we must give him such faith as we may have. It may be little, but give it to him. Reach for him out of the anonymous crowd. Pull the tassel of his garment. You might even hear him say: "Your faith has saved you; go in peace."

JESUS
AND THE HUNGRY

There could be seen along the roads of old Palestine a common and pitiable sight. It was the beggar, hungry and destitute, reaching out emaciated hands for help. "Bread, bread, give us bread, for pity's sake give us bread." Jesus heard the cry, saw the suffering, for was he not brought up among the poor? He sensed an even deeper hunger in those about him, the hunger of man's spirit for the eternal, for God. So to supply bread for the body, and bread for the soul, became a supreme passion of his life.

There are several stories that show Christ's concern for the hunger of the body. There is the strange, vivid incident of the feeding of a crowd of five thousand people by the Sea of Galilee. Apparently it was a story of great significance for the disciples of the early church. It is the only incident, apart from happenings in the last week of the life of Jesus, recounted in all four Gospels.

Jesus comes across the Sea of Galilee, only to find crowds waiting for him on the other shore. Moving a little inland, he speaks to them throughout the remainder of the day. As evening comes, he senses in the restlessness of the people the pangs of hunger. With compassion he turns to his disciples, "How are we to buy bread, so that these people may eat?" Philip tells him that to spend as much as two hundred denarii —about forty-five dollars today—would be virtually useless. I expect this was the total resources in the treasury of that little disciple band. The disciples had a simple solution—send the people away to fend for themselves.

Somehow a small boy gets into the picture. "There is a lad here who has five barley loaves and two fishes; but what are they among so many?" Jesus takes the food from the boy, gives thanks to God for his goodness, and then distributes it to the disciples.

Then the Bible records one of the strange miracle stories of Jesus. The food, so meager, is multiplied. As the disciples pass through the crowds seated on the ground, there is enough bread and fish for all. Indeed beyond the satisfaction of the hunger of the crowd, much is left over. "Gather up the fragments left over, that nothing may be lost," said Jesus. Twelve baskets full of fragments remained. No wonder the people said in astonishment: "This is indeed the Prophet who is to come into the world."

Jesus helped people who were hungry by placing their need at the center of his consciousness and accepting responsibility for it. Like the disciples of old, we would prefer to send the hungry away to fend for themselves. Jesus confronts us with his probing question, "How are we to buy bread so that these people may eat?"

We know how intensely Jesus felt the hunger of the people because of what happened at the beginning of his public ministry. Learning that the time had come for him to leave the security of Nazareth and to begin the work for which he was born, Jesus went onto the plateau above Jericho to choose the method he would adopt in his ministry. There, lonely and wrestling, these words reached his ears, "Turn these stones into bread." In these words was the challenge to become a social reformer, to set out to grapple primarily with the social and economic needs of the world. Jesus rejected this way of direct social action. But the material need of people took its place in a larger vision and in a purpose that went deeper than man's body. There was no rejection of the demands of the body. Jesus was

42

never able to turn a deaf ear to the cry: "Bread, bread, for pity's sake give us bread."

The living Christ today is placing the cry of the people for bread at the center of the conscience of mankind. He is not allowing us to push the hungry crowds away. How do we know? It is seen in the concern rising in his church and in the world at large for those who are hungry. The great division of Inter-church Aid of the World Council of Churches, with its massive response to hunger wherever it is found, is evidence of the reality of his call. The ministry of the Spirit of Jesus is always to be seen far beyond the boundaries of his church. So it is in these years that the Freedom from Hunger Campaign has gripped the imagination of millions. Jesus is aiding the hungry by placing their need on the heart of mankind.

The cry for bread rises more consistently and in more volume today than ever in history. Look at the facts. Two thirds of the people of the world are underfed. Hundreds of millions of people go to bed hungry most nights, in all their days scarcely knowing what we in the affluent West would call a square meal. Most of these families are forced to live on an income that represents a purchasing power of about $1.50 per week.

The blunt truth is that the world hunger situation is getting worse. The staggering "population explosion" of our time is outstripping every effort to keep pace with it. Think of these statistics. In the days of Jesus there were approximately 250 million people in the world. It took until 1650 for that population to double to 500 million. Then the whole scene changed. By 1850, only 200 years later, population had doubled again. By 1950 it was up to 2½ billion. Now it has reached 3 billion people, and if present trends continue, it will be only 30 years, that is 1990, before there will be 6 billion people around the world clamoring to be fed. Every single day now the population of the world is increasing by 140,000 babies. Never in all history has such a situation confronted mankind.

In the face of multiplying people, what is the answer? Great developmental programs are inescapable. Improvements in agriculture, the lifting of production by industrial expansion, the shifting of people from overcrowded and exhausted fields to empty lands like Australia, must all go forward. New plans for world food distribution which will end the scandal of bursting storehouses of surpluses in America, while people are dying daily of starvation in India, must be fashioned. Yet all this is not sufficient. As the United Nations has declared: "World food production is lagging behind population growth, so there is less food per person as the days go by."

Recently I was in India and I saw the problem in its starkest terms. India, in seeking to lift the standards of its people, has launched its successive five-year plans of expansion. A five-year period has recently drawn to a close, and expansion industrially and in food production has been achieved. However, a census was taken while I was in India, and it was found that many more children had been born in this period than had been expected. The rate of population growth proved to be greater than the expansion of productivity. The result was that all efforts were being absorbed not in advancing but in scarcely maintaining present standards of living. Hence the disturbing fact emerges: that unless in India the present birthrate can be reduced, the population will double every twenty-three years, creating a deepening crisis.

What is the answer? There is but one solution. It is to carry through a worldwide family planning and birth control campaign. There is no other answer to the growing overpopulation of the world.

Unless ways can be found of reducing population, every gain in food production and industrial expansion will be nullified.

Australia, the United States, and Great Britain, through the United Nations, should today be subsidizing great worldwide family planning educational crusades. They should be making grants to enable the people of poorer nations to obtain scientific means of controlling births. Steadily the idea should be transmitted that the day is coming when to have more than four or five children will be regarded as irresponsible, even a crime against humanity. No heed must be given to reactionary forces which would impede human progress. The Roman Catholic Church, by opposing scientific means of controlling birth, is doing a great disservice to humanity. This obstruction is far more serious than the earlier blunders of the church in scientific obscurantism, for it could cause untold suffering to an ever increasing mass of people. Now, not later, is the hour for action. The conclusion of Richard M. Fagley is inescapable: "No strategy of development can succeed without a fairly rapid as well as massive extension of family limitation in some form."

How does God, through his Son Jesus Christ, help the hungry? He does it by the miracle of the multiplication of food.

There are many difficulties connected with the story of the feeding of the five thousand. Many ingenious explanations have been given to try to explain the central mystery of what happened. None is convincing. The biblical account is clear. It presents the story as a clear-cut miracle, wrought by Jesus in the face of the need of the people, and accepted by them as a startling sign that the Promised One, the Messiah for whom they had looked, had come.

Let us for a moment turn our gaze away from the scene at Galilee. Harvest time always presents the miracle of the multiplication of food. The waving wheat fields, the brown husks hiding the golden grain, the wool waiting to be shorn, the vegetables of the garden, and the fruit of the orchard, all declare God's constant miracle of multiplication of food for the feeding of his people.

It is easy to forget the miracle God performs through

natural creation. Daniel Evans once imagined a man living in an isolated place in a forest to which no other person, as far as he knew, ever came. Every day, however, when he left his home, something would happen. He would discover when he returned flowers on the table in his room and a basket of food at his door. He was never able to discover the identity of the one who brought gifts to his home. He inferred, and surely rightly so, that there was another person around, whose attitude toward him was one of friendly goodwill.

Every day a basket of food is placed upon our table. Every day flowers are available to make beautiful our home. We may rightly believe that there is Someone around whose intention for us is good.

> Back of the loaf is the snowy flour,
> And back of the flour the mill,
> And back of the mill is the wheat and the shower
> And the sun and the Father's will.

This then is a miracle, if we had but eyes to see it. God, our Heavenly Father, constantly satisfies our hunger by the miracle of the multiplication of food.

Now if Jesus is God present among us, is it not reasonable to expect him to be able to carry out creative acts similar to those with which we have become familiar over the years? William Temple poses the issue clearly: "If Jesus was indeed God Incarnate the story of the feeding of the five thousand presents no insuperable difficulties. But, of course, such a creative act is made quite incredible if He is other or less than God Incarnate."

Therefore, as we think of the miracle beside Galilee, we find ourselves once again facing Jesus Christ. Is he just another of the prophets, though perhaps the best of them all? Is he the unique Son of God? Do we call him teacher and example, or bow at his feet as Lord and God? These are the questions we must answer as we stand puzzling about the miracle of the feeding of the five thousand.

Who is this Jesus? Carl Adam makes us face him: "An awe-inspiring figure is the Christ of the Gospels, planted like a tremendous mystery in our midst. He stands forth challengingly, a riddle which must be solved, a question which must be answered."

Each man and woman must answer personally. I can only tell of my own reply. I must say:

> If Jesus Christ is a man—
> And only a man,—I say
> That of all mankind I cleave to him,
> And to him will I cleave alway.
>
> If Jesus Christ is a God—
> And the only God,—I swear
> I will follow him through heaven and hell,
> The earth, the sea, the air.

How does Jesus help the hungry? By performing the miracle of sharing with us whatever we place in his hands.

I wonder if you have ever tried to look at the incident of the feeding of the five thousand through the eyes of the small boy. How excited he must have been that night when at last he reached home. I can imagine him saying to his mother, "I followed Jesus as closely as I could. I was so near I could hear him talking to his disciples. I heard him say, "How are we to buy bread so that these people may eat?" The disciples suggested sending the people away, but Jesus wanted to help them. I heard Jesus ask whether there was any food among the crowd. It was then that I went to Andrew and said I had five loaves and two fish. Andrew spoke to Jesus and then Jesus came over to me. I gave him all I had and I watched him as he held it up and prayed. It was a wonderful prayer, for it seemed as if he were really talking to God. Then he broke the five loaves in two and gave a piece to ten of the disciples. To the other two he gave a fish each. They went out through the crowd, handing out from baskets into which they had put the food, a little to everybody. They seemed to go on and on, and whenever they placed their hands in the basket more food was there. At last it was over and Jesus came over to me. He thanked me and then said, 'You will always be willing to share what you have, my son?' And then he smiled at me. Mother, I shall remember his smile as long, as long as I shall live."

If you find difficulty in believing that food was multiplied as the story says, then at least you may surely believe this interpretation. It is a story built on the miracle of what sharing can do. Perhaps, as some have suggested, the miracle was no more than Jesus calling on all who had brought food to share it with those around them. Certainly it is inconceivable that the boy near him was the only one who had shown some foresight in bringing food to that lonely place. Perhaps it was nothing more than a miracle of sharing.

The real sin in the present hunger crisis of the world is the failure to share. The United States has its storehouses bursting with surplus farm products. Huge sums are being expended annually in storage charges. Somehow, no one cares enough to distribute the surpluses of the United States amid the want of India. Australia lies on the edge of Asia. It is a huge empty continent. It could be a great food bowl of Asia. Australia lives to itself in two ways. It has a restrictive immigration policy which forbids Asians from settling in Australia where food may be found and food may be grown. It also limits the amount of wheat that can be sown on farms. There are even benighted politicians who object to wheat being sold to China, which is regarded by them as a possible, potential enemy.

The distribution of all surpluses and the cultivation of all Australia may not make an appreciable difference to world hunger, and such steps would in no sense be a sufficient, permanent solution. But hungry people are people. The multitudes that cry out for bread are made up of a child here, an anxious mother there, and a

hungry father unable to gain employment. Millions
would be saved the pangs of hunger if only we would
offer our five loaves and two fish to our neighbor. Jesus
could feed some of the hungry if we would but enter
with him into the miracle of sharing.

The world is full of stories showing what God can
do with a little. As G. H. C. Macgregor says in com-
menting on this very miracle: "Christ is shown to be
one who produces mighty results from the slenderest
possible means."

There has appeared no greater Christian in this century than Toyohiko Kagawa of Japan. His whole life
is evidence of what God can do with a little, when that
little is placed in his hands. Kagawa was in Kobe when
the great earthquake of 1923 struck Japan. Soon the
terrible news filtered through. Tokyo was almost destroyed. There were 5,000,000 homeless, 100,000 dead.
Fire and a tidal wave had completed the destruction
begun with the quaking of the earth. Quietly Kagawa
said to his wife, "I must go to Tokyo. At once!" Without any idea of what he could do, Kagawa reached the
capital of Japan. There he found officials stupified by
the shock of what had happened. No plan seemed to be
emerging. Back he went to Kobe. He collected a great
supply of food, clothes, and bedding. He hired a deep-
sea fishing vessel and sailed up the coast to Tokyo. He
established relief centers to which the people could
come. Soon he was noticed by a government groping
for answers to disaster. Impressed by his shrewd ability

51

the prime minister added him to an imperial economic commission. He was the only man chosen from the ranks of the people. So rehabilitation schemes took shape. Kagawa was not alone responsible for them, but no one will deny that the inspiration and wisdom he gave were incalculable. Kagawa shared his all with God, and God worked his ancient miracle of multiplying that which was put in his hand.

"How are we able to buy bread, so that these people may eat?" How? By people like you and me coming forward and sharing such talents and dedication as we may have. Almost ashamed we shrink back, saying, "What is so little to God?" We have forgotten the miracle God can work when we share with him such resources as we have. Still Jesus wants to feed the hungry round the world, through someone in helplessness giving all he has to him.

How does Jesus help the hungry? He does it by meeting the deepest hunger of all, the hunger of mankind for the bread of life.

No one should read the sixth chapter of John without seeing it in its wholeness. This wonderful chapter begins with the story of the feeding of the crowd of five thousand who were physically hungry beside the Sea of Galilee. It ends with Christ speaking of his coming death, of his body to be broken for men, and of the satisfaction men would find as they ate of his flesh and drank of his blood. Quietly, he tells of the food which he alone can give. "I am the living bread which came down from Heaven; if any one eats of this bread, he will live for ever."

It was Jesus who, while ever conscious of those whose bodies were hungry, repeated the great words of the Old Testament, "Man shall not live by bread alone." He spoke no more penetrating word. The lives of so many of us and the present picture of the total life of the affluent lands of western culture prove how right he was. Most of us in lands such as Sweden, Great Britain, the United States, Canada, Australia, never know what it feels like to be really hungry. Yet is our plentiful supply of bread enough? The hearts of so many of us are empty, and life has lost any sense of satisfaction. Our cultures are shot through with unsolved problems. Our cities and our towns are filled with distracted, unhappy people. Divorce, alcoholism, child delinquency, and suicide, all bear obvious witness to the simple truth that man cannot live by bread alone.

Why cannot we see it? Man is more than what he eats. Because we are more than body, ordinary bread will never be enough. We are so made that every part of us must be nourished. If our bodies are not fed with food, they shrink and die. If our minds receive no stimulus of thought or education, they become limited and closed. If our imaginations are undernourished, life loses its wonder and its joy. If our emotions lack love, something within us dies. If our spirits are not fed with the grace of God, they perish. The blunt truth is that with millions of people today souls and spirits are underfed and starved as much as bodies were in the bad old days of our western society. This is the measure of our tragedy today.

There appeared at the Sydney Central Methodist Mission one Sunday night a striking Australian girl. Sunday by Sunday she came, sitting alone. Gradually we got to know her and learned that she was but eighteen years of age, and that she had left her northern home for what she believed would be the exciting life of a great city. Already she had been in difficulty with the police. Already she had moved far from the piety of a mother and father who continued to pray for her. Always I shall remember the night when, in answer to an appeal for lives to be given to Christ, she came forward, simply, boldly. This began a new chapter, a chapter of redemption. It began also years of witness and service to Christ. God used the very experiences she had passed through to give added power to her witness.

A year after her conversion she stood one night in the Sydney town hall and told her story to two thousand young people at a great youth rally.

"Before I was sixteen I had run away from home, been before the children's court, and put on probation till I was eighteen," she said quietly. "Between the ages of sixteen and seventeen I was in and out of trouble with the police and thought I was a big-time baddie. The day after I turned eighteen I left home to come and live in Sydney. At last my dreams had come true, I could live my life the way I wanted to. So my life began in the big city which for so many years had been the Shangri-La of my dreams.

"It took me exactly four months to become so disillusioned with life I didn't care if I lived or died. In those four months I and the girl I was living with did all those things I thought would be so great. I saw Palmer Street at night, watched some strippers in action, watched people play the poker machines. We also knew men who wanted us to live with or work for them.

"Then Christ took a hand in the direction of my life. I had heard about the service in the Lyceum Theater. I came alone. By this time I was so confused about what was right and wrong I didn't know where I was, but the service was on the Ten Commandments and Christ spoke to me through that service.

"There was no sudden shining light as far as I was concerned, but that night there was the awakening somewhere within me, something that was real, with depth in it. For a time I used to go to church then on to a dance, and I still mixed with my old friends. However, a gradual change was taking place. I started to notice that beyond the bright lights of the nightclubs there was a beauty these would never match—trees, flowers, sunsets, and sea. I started to think of people, and wonder who could have made such intricate beings. So, I began to believe in a god, a supreme being, someone worthy of human worship.

"Slowly I came to think not of "a" god, but "the" God, my Heavenly Father, someone not beyond my reach, but someone who knew and cared about me. I don't mean my life is just one happy picnic. I get cross, irritable, and discouraged. But I am happier than I have ever been since I let Christ be the one to exercise discipline over me. I am now a member of the Central Methodist Mission, am living the happiest, fullest life I have yet experienced, and am more content than I have ever been, thanks to the change Christ has brought to my life."

Hungry? One stands among us who still says quietly, "I am the living bread which came down from heaven; if anyone eats of this bread he will live for ever."

JESUS
AND THE MEN WHO
WERE AFRAID

"There is one universal passion: it is fear," says George Bernard Shaw. He is right. Every one of us knows what it is to be afraid.

From millions of lives fear is filching happiness. With some of us fear reaches out of the past, its dead, clammy hand spoiling the present. With others it is fear of today, of the perils of hour-by-hour living which curses our path. Yet again there are those of us who dread the future. We are so obsessed by what may happen tomorrow we cannot live at peace with ourselves today.

The name of our fears is legion. Fear of sickness, of unemployment, of social rejection, of war, of sin, of loneliness, of not getting married, of old age, of death, of judgment, of hell, march through the minds and emotions of modern people. Somehow, somewhere, if life is to be good, we must find an answer to fear.

There is a wonderful story in the Gospel of Mark of how Jesus calmed his men when they were afraid. It happened this way. One evening Jesus announced to his men that they would set out from where they had been working across the Sea of Galilee to the Capernaum side of the lake. They entered a small boat and, accompanied by several other boats, were soon well out from the shore. Jesus, exhausted, fell asleep as the disciples rowed.

Suddenly a storm arose. Galilee is a small, freshwater lake. It is only thirteen miles long and eight miles wide. It is fashioned almost in the shape of a heart. The hills and valleys around it seem to make almost a funnel which points at the lake. From this formation sudden, fierce storms can devolep, with waves up to thirty feet high being whipped up quickly.

Struck by one of these sudden storms, the disciples panicked. As their small boat started to ship water they wakened Jesus saying, "Do you not care if we perish?" The story says Jesus rebuked the wind and said to the sea, "Peace! Be still!" As suddenly as the storm had come it was gone, and there was a great calm.

Then Jesus turned on his men. "Why are you afraid? Have you no faith?" The awestruck disciples had no answer. They could only say in wonder: "Who then is this, that even wind and sea obey him?"

Over all the centuries people have seen in the storm on Galilee a symbol of the storms which can sweep through the human heart. Suddenly disaster can strike. There come the moments when the waves of sin or suffering or sorrow seem certain to overwhelm life.

As Master of the storms of life stands Jesus. We see him rebuking the forces which would destroy us. To the quaking heart he brings peace. To the fearful life he carries faith. In the story of the storm on Galilee, we see how Jesus helps people who are afraid.

Jesus calms our fears by declaring that this is God's world. By showing us that God is our Heavenly Father, fear of what might happen to us is hushed.

What a picture of faith, as of a child, is given with Jesus quietly sleeping while a storm raged. All were resting in God his Father's hand, so Jesus could sleep on without fear.

There are two kinds of fears which gnaw at us. One is the specific fear. We can give it a name. It is focused and definite. The other is the vague, general fear of we know not what. Each has to be faced in a different way, yet each has to be conquered if we are to know peace.

We all know something of the specific fears which from time to time well up in our lives. We suffer a hidden pain and fear it might point to a deadly disease. We hear a noise in the night and are sure it is a burglar. We dread the results of an examination in which we think we did poorly. We are frightened we may not be able to measure up to some particular task ahead.

There is only one way to find victory over particular fears—to face them. Fear is able to blackmail us because it remains in the shadows. To bring it into the open, to look it squarely in the face, is to rob it of its power.

From the life of Francis of Assisi comes a great story of triumph over fear. Francis had a deep fear of leprosy. One day when riding outside the walls of Assisi, he saw a leper coming toward him. He knew at once his courage was challenged.

G. K. Chesterton in his biography of Francis tells us what happened.

Francis saw his fear coming up the road towards him; the fear that comes from within not from without; though it stood white and horrible in the sunlight.

For once in the rush of his life his soul must have stood still. Then he sprang from his horse and rushed on the leper and threw his arms around him. To this man he gave what money he could and mounted and rode on. We do not know how far he rode, or with what sense of the things around him; but it is said that when he looked back, he could see no figure on the road.

He could see no figure on the road! That is what happens when we face many of the specific fears which lurk within us. They vanish from sight.

Much more difficult to silence are the fears which are vague and indefinite. We are fearful just of living. We read of tragedy striking at the children of other homes. We imagine what we would do if an automobile accident took from our side the ones we love. We live, in a time of economic recession, with fear of unemployment. Across our world lies the mushroom shadow of the cloud which rises from the bursting atomic bomb, and fear of war clutches at our hearts.

The answer to the uneasy fear is faith, faith in the goodness of God, faith in the providential care of our Heavenly Father. It is this kind of faith which allowed Jesus to sleep without fear amid the storm on Galilee.

This is God's world. It does not belong to man. It has not fallen into the hands of the devil. It is not an orphan world belonging to nobody. God is the owner and ruler of all things. As the Negro spiritual puts it: "He's got the whole world in his hands."

This is God's world because he made it. From his mind has flowed the vast design of the universe, from his creative power everything has come into being. The almost infinite distances of space, the intricate coordination of nature, the providential supplying of the needs of man, have all come from God.

This is God's world because he redeemed it. God has claimed this world as his own by coming in Jesus Christ and dwelling among us. He has an undeniable stake in history. It takes the form of a jagged cross driven hard into the earth at a place called Calvary. The world is twice God's; he made it and he redeemed it.

This is God's world because he is at work in it today. His Spirit strives in history and within individual lives to fulfill his purposes. There is always an unknown factor in every situation; it is the presence and operation of the Holy Spirit.

This is God's world because one day he will claim it as his own, gathering the world in triumph to himself. God, who began history, will end it. There will be an end to human history just as every single life comes to a close in death. That end will not be caused by the foolishness or wickedness of man, but by God. The end of history will be the triumph of his kingdom when at last we shall understand how much God loves the world.

We can interpret all that happens to us in the light of this full-orbed faith of a Christian. In such a context our vague, general fears can subside. With quiet confidence we can face the present and the future unafraid. There are solid grounds for saying:

> Always hath the daylight broken
> Always hath the comfort spoken
> Better hath He been for years
> Than our fears.

There is a notable sentence in the Bible which says: "Perfect love casts out fear." It is a sense of the tender, caring love of God that drives away fear.

Jesus revealed to the world the tremendous fact of

the love of God. He lived by that love, walking day by day without fear. To him it was inconceivable that anyone should ask the question spoken by the frightened disciples in the boat: "Teacher, do you not care if we perish?"

Why, of course Jesus cared. And God always cares. His love encompasses us all, holding us personally, individually, within his providence.

Fear is of course an emotion. This is why it so often cannot be overcome by reason or argument. We may be completely convinced intellectually that there is nothing to fear, yet in the next moment we can be stricken with dread.

Only an emotion can really cast out an emotion. This is why love is needed to deal with fear. Love can overthrow fear, for love too is based in the emotions.

There was a striking illustration given of the power of love in an incident which occurred at Malmesbury. A circus came to town, and a mother took her little girl to see the lions and the tigers. The mother's attention wandered for a few minutes, and when she looked around she was horrified to see her small child had slipped through the bars into the lion's cage.

Without a moment's hesitation the mother threw open the door of the cage, rushed in, and literally pulled her child from the lion's claws. Then she turned, slammed the door shut in the lion's face, and fainted.

Now that woman feared lions as much as you and I do. For the moment, however, love cast out fear. The emotion of love for her little girl gave her courage to enter a lion's cage. Love silenced fear.

It is only the perfect love of God which casts out all fear. The love of a wife or husband, the love of parent or child, can overcome some fear. But human love is always less than perfect love. Only the love of God silences all our fears.

How do we know God is love? We become certain of it because of Jesus. Herbert Farmer puts it well in his book *God and Men*.

Discerning the love of God at work at that one point in historical time, the Christian is prepared to trust it over all history, all time; discerning it at that one point in space, he is prepared to trust it—as it were—in all places whatsoever, and over all space; discerning it at work in that particular complex of personal relationships which constitutes the earthly life of Jesus, he is prepared to trust it to be at work in all personal relationships whatsoever.

The wonder of the ever-flowing love of God swept over me when I stood one day at Victoria Falls in Central Africa. The African people call the falls "the smoke that thunders." The name comes from the way the mile-wide Zambezi River thunders into the gorge, sending vast billows of spray high in the air.

As I stood watching the falls, I suddenly realized that no doubt one hundred thousand years ago, when the so-called Broken Hill man looked on them, the waters flowed. I remembered waking in the night in our camp and hearing the roar from the gorge and thinking, while I slept the waters flowed. We journeyed some distance into Northern Rhodesia and looked back and could see the spray billowing above the trees—whereever we went the waters flowed on.

Suddenly it all became a picture for me of the love of God. Long before I was born, and after I am gone, the love of God flows on. When I am asleep, when I am awake, and love of God is there. When I think of that love, when I forget it, that love remains. Nothing, nothing can stop the love of God coursing through the world he has made. Oh, the wonder, the glory of the love of God! To think of it, to accept it, is to lose all fear.

Jesus helps us to conquer fear because his authority stretches over all things. He has not only the will but the power to say to our fearful hearts: "Peace! Be still!"

I wonder if you have noticed a significant fact about the storm on Galilee. It says that when Jesus was awakened, "he rebuked the wind." He began by coming to grips with the cause of the waves. He dealt with causes, not effects. So not to the boisterous waves does he first turn, but to the cause of them, the wind. "He rebuked the wind."

What a commanding figure Jesus must have presented in that small boat. He rebuked the wind and said, "Peace! Be still!" There followed a great calm. No wonder the disciples said: "Who then is this, that even wind and sea obey him?"

Peace of heart remains the great need of our time. Noel Coward in his play *Design for Living* points to a significant fact. One of his characters complains that amid all the inventions of this twentieth century no one has created anything "to create quiet and calm."

Perhaps no such invention has been found because it is not needed. Jesus has come, and Jesus has the power to surround all our lives with the peace of God. Who can be blamed save ourselves if we accept it not?

Godfrey Thring, the hymn writer, tells us what is available to us as we live in turmoil and danger from the storms of life.

> The wild winds hushed; the angry deep
> Sank, like a little child, to sleep;
> The sullen billows ceased to leap,
>   At thy will.
> So, when our life is clouded o'er
> And storm-winds drift us from the shore,
> Say, lest we sink to rise no more,
>   "Peace, be still."

Nothing appeals to me more in the story of the storm on Galilee than this simple statement: "He rebuked the wind." Here is the realism of Christ. He goes down to the cause of things. He removes fear by coming to grips with the forces which create fear.

It is at this point that the Christian church has so often been less creative and effective than its Lord. The church has a great record of bringing relief to those in need, of easing human suffering. It has a less significant history in dealing with the causes of suffering. It has too often been content to operate an ambulance service at the foot of a cliff, rather than agitating to have a fence built at the top of the precipice. It has too often been satisfied to substitute charity for justice. It has too often tried to deal with the waves, rather than the wind that causes them.

Take, for example, the question of the vast world problem of alcoholism. It is a gain to see that the moment has come when alcoholism is treated as a disease rather than a sin. It is good that rehabilitation centers are appearing round the world to try to heal the broken life of the alcoholic.

But is this all that should be done? What about the breweries? What about the endless advertising of alcoholic beverages? What about the conditions under which alcohol is sold? Has the church nothing to say there?

The real cause of the fear which lives in the hearts of the wives and children of many an alcoholic home is the industry which manufactures and peddles intoxicating liquor. Jesus rebuked the wind. Perhaps there is his realism in the attitude of the Methodist Church of Australia, the declared position of which is "unswerving hostility to the liquor trade."

Again, look at the world problem of racialism. Recently in South Africa I was appalled at the unnecessary hurt and suffering which the government's policy of apartheid creates. The closer one gets to this iniquitous expression of racialism, the worse it looks. This is because of the way it falls as a crushing burden on little people whose skins happen to be dark.

I was not twenty-four hours in South Africa before government officials wanted to show me the vast new African "locations" or housing areas on the outskirts of Johannesburg. Then almost pathetically they waited to hear a comment of commendation.

I could only say that if the new housing areas were for slum clearance alone, there could be nothing but praise. But they are linked with the policy of apartheid. They are based on legislation which demands segregation, which denies Africans ever to own even the small house in which they live. Therefore it seemed to me only one comment was valid: "Benign policies of charity can never be a substitute for justice."

There will be no peace in South Africa or anywhere else while the evils of conscious racialism remain. It is the wind, not the waves, which cries out for rebuke. Only a church which in South Africa "rebukes the wind,"—racialism itself—will ever silence the fears which ride in men's hearts.

Jesus rebuked the wind. Then the waves subsided. To this ministry he calls us. As we respond in faith and obedience, then and only then will there come the calm of a society in which justice reigns.

The New Testament declares the faith that Christ is Master of the storm. The winds and the waves do indeed obey Him. In matchless language Paul declares that God has placed Christ "far above all rule and authority and power and dominion, . . . and has put all things under his feet."

From the long annals of history comes many a story which proves the ascendancy of Christ. So powerful have been the winds and the waves of evil that to hope for their conquest seemed absurd. But in Christ's name men have witnessed and prayed, have often died that righteousness might abound. And the victory has surely come.

The South African author Alan Paton has a moving end to his book *Cry, the Beloved Country.* He knows not when the full day of justice, liberty, and equality will come to all the people of his land. All he knows is that that day will come.

His faith is expressed in the coming of the dawn among the hills. He describes how the mountain tops first catch the light of the rising sun. Then it moves steadily down into the darkened valleys, penetrating into the blackest corners.

"For," he says, "it is the dawn that has come, as it has come for a thousand centuries, never failing. But when that dawn will come, of our emancipation, from the fear of bondage and the bondage of fear, why, that is a secret."

Jesus helps us to conquer fear, fear which rises from the storms of life. Why? Above all else, because he has the power to rebuke the wind!

JESUS
AND A SUICIDE

Jesus lost his man. This is the startling fact which comes from the story of the most famous suicide of all history. Jesus was unable to save Judas Iscariot from base betrayal, and he failed to relieve Judas' black despair which came with the realization of what he had done and which drove him to self-destruction. Hence a simple, stark sentence ends the life story of Judas: "And Judas went and hanged himself."

70

Today suicide is a vast world problem. In country after country the number of people who no longer find life worth living is increasing. In Greater London about 3 people commit suicide each day. Almost as many people die by their own hands, approximately 5,000 annually, as died in road accidents in England and Wales. It is impossible to know accurately how many attempt suicide and fail, but some say 40,000 attempts in England and Wales are made every year.

In the United States about 60 people commit suicide daily. The suicide rate is increasing in Australia, 1,249 killing themselves in 1961. A recent World Health Organization statement listed, in order, the countries where the suicide rate is highest: West Berlin, East Germany, Hungary, Austria, Finland, Switzerland, Japan, and Denmark. At least 250,000 men and women round the world end their lives each year by suicide.

How did Jesus try to help Judas Iscariot? If we can see how Jesus attempted to save Judas from himself, even though he failed, we may discover how he can help us today.

In the New Testament story Judas briefly but vividly passes before us. As with the other eleven disciples, Jesus chose Judas to be with him. He must have seen the potential greatness of Judas, and Judas at that time responded gladly and hopefully.

In the disciple band Judas gained prominence, being made treasurer. It is in his handling of money that we are given a first glimpse that all is not well in his life.

He is labeled a thief for using for his own ends money which belonged to all.

Gradually light turns to darkness in the soul of Judas. Soon he is a traitor, in league with the enemies of Jesus. He agrees for thirty pieces of silver—the value of a slave—to lead the soldiers of the high priest to a place where Jesus could be arrested quietly.

Following his successful betrayal, remorse overwhelms Judas. With gathering momentum the tragedy moves toward its climax. Distraught, Judas returns to the men who had bought him, but from them gained no sympathy. In the sheer despair of that hour there seemed no way out save suicide.

A first clue to an understanding of the tragedy of Judas comes from his relationship with the other disciples. Judas, says the story, was a man from Kerioth. This means he was the only Judean, or southerner, amid the disciples, all the rest of whom came from the north.

It is amazing how often antagonism develops between southern and northern people. Possibly the division in the disciple band caused Judas to develop loneliness. Sensing his difference in outlook and temperament he began perhaps to draw back within himself. The feeling of alienation and rejection deepened as he suffered real and imaginary slights from the others. The seeds of the bitterness which led to his ultimate betrayal of Jesus could easily have been sown in the loneliness of that different man, the man from Kerioth.

No crime of all history has been so often and so

closely examined as Judas' betrayal of Jesus. Yet no one can state with confidence what was the motive which drove him to his infamous act. And now we shall never know with any certainty, for we probably have all the facts we shall ever have.

The simple, surface explanation is that Judas betrayed Jesus for thirty pieces of silver. Certainly this is the view hinted at in John 12:6: "He was a thief, and as he had the money box he used to take what was put into it." Love of money took possession of him until it destroyed him. It may seem superficial to suggest the motive of greed, and anyway the money received was so little that it could scarcely have satisfied greed.

It could be that the simple explanation is the right one. Behind so many of the crimes of society is lust for money. Often heinous evil is committed for the sake of small financial gain. Love of money can become so great that even for a little of it large sacrifices of honor and integrity are made.

I have never found convincing the more fanciful theories used to explain the actions of Judas. Judas never really meant Jesus to die, it is said. He was merely trying to force Jesus to show his hand, to claim his kingdom. Then events got out of hand, and Judas killed himself because of the complete failure of his plans.

Eric Waterhouse, in his little book *What Is Salvation?* gives the most satisfying analysis of Judas I have ever read. Waterhouse claims there is all the evidence of deep and involved psychological problems behind Judas' final betrayal of Jesus.

Judas, he claims, began with enthusiasm as a disciple. Then disappointment with Jesus, and alienation from the other disciples, brought a cooling off of allegiance. Then, unhappy, all manner of words and actions began to irritate and annoy him. "Just as air means life to the living and decay to the dead," says Dr. Waterhouse, "so the presence of Jesus which gives life to the living soul, hastened the moral decay of Judas."

Judas, however, had to live with himself. He could do this only by finding a scapegoat, by throwing the blame on someone else. By projecting his own inner declension and unhappiness onto Jesus, he escaped conscious self-condemnation. Judas, though he did not know it, began to hate Jesus because he hated himself.

Hatred is never rational, be it in the mind of the assassin of a president or the betrayer of Jesus. Bitterness takes over and is satisfied only by the destruction of the object of the hatred. So the blackest deed of the centuries was finally enacted.

Shining through the blackness of the story of Judas are the steadfast love and patience of Jesus. We see Jesus again and again trying to save Judas from himself.

Jesus tried to cling to Judas. Although he must have sensed Judas was near to betrayal point, he did not exclude him from the Last Supper. Throughout that meal there appears more than once an appeal to Judas, at the last hour, to abandon his plot. At last the break came, and Judas hurried from the lighted room into the darkness.

I once saw a painting of the departure of Judas. He can be seen hurrying across a beam of light which is streaming through a window of the room he had just left. With bitter face he can be seen looking back. Jesus is standing at the head of the table, looking with infinite compassion and mute appeal at Judas. When Jesus looked at Peter in the judgment hall, that look almost broke his heart and he went out and wept bitterly. When Jesus looked at Judas it failed; Judas hurried on to betrayal.

Jesus made one further effort to redeem Judas from destruction. It was in the Garden of Gethsemane. Judas has arrived with the soldiers. He steps forward in the darkness to give the prearranged signal as to which of the shadowy figures is Jesus. Then is given the most hypocritical kiss of all time.

And Jesus? What does he say? "Friend." At such a moment he says: "Friend, why are you here?"

Rendel Harris says that archaeologists have found a number of drinking cups belonging to the first century which have on them the words spoken by Jesus to Judas: "Friend, why art thou come hither?" Then appear two further words: "Be Merry."

Could it be that such a cup was used by Jesus at the Last Supper? If it was, Jesus was still subtly struggling to pull Judas back from destruction. He was reminding him of the cup from which they had both drunk, and recalling the fellowship of the disciple band. Jesus was trying to tell Judas that there still was time to repent, that he could still take his place among the disciples. "Friend, why are you here?"

Jesus is here wrestling with the dark mood of the mental and emotional distortions of a man on the road to destruction. He is using the only appeal which might penetrate. Moral judgment, criticism, condemnation would only deepen the sickness. Love might heal and save. So Jesus offers to Judas love's last appeal.

All is of no avail. Judas moves on to the prearranged climax. Jesus is arrested, tried, condemned, crucified. As for Judas it had still to be written: "Judas went out, and it was night."

The suicide of Judas, the final act in the grim drama, was an act of sheer despair. Realizing at last the enormity of what he had done, he could no longer sustain the burden of guilt. He could see but one way out, and he took it. Judas went and hanged himself.

The condemnation of Jesus to death seems to have been the act which at long last revealed Judas to himself. Suddenly he realized that Jesus was not the Jesus he had previously seen through the distorting haze of his own bitterness and hatred.

Judas rushed to the high priest and tried to undo what he had done. "I have sinned," he distraughtly sobbed, "in betraying innocent blood." But there are some things which cannot be undone. It was a foolish, vain hope to think the men who had cold-bloodedly plotted the destruction of Jesus and used Judas as a pawn would repent. So they scornfully said: "What is that to us?"

Now Judas could not bear to retain the coins. Throwing them at his tormentors' feet, he rushed from their presence. Within a little time, with despair complete, Judas embraced a suicide's death.

The black loneliness and despair which surround death by suicide were illustrated to me by an event in Sydney. Through it, I think, I was given new insight and sympathy for the man of Kerioth, who in complete aloneness slipped a rope's noose over his own head somewhere in Jerusalem.

Late one Saturday night my telephone rang. Quietly a man's voice began to unfold his intention to commit suicide. For an hour I wrestled with him over that phone. He would only give his Christian name, Roy, and would not disclose his address. He was an utter failure, he said. He had written me a letter which I would receive on Monday morning. "By then," he said, "I will be dead."

At last, failing to gain his name or address I invited him to come to worship the next day. "I happen to be speaking on 'Life's Glorious Failures' tomorrow night. Please come. God might speak to you if you will listen." Then suddenly the phone clicked, and he was gone.

That Sunday night I preached with an added sense of responsibility. During the early part of the service I scanned the faces of the people. Was Roy there? If he was, I knew I was contending for a man's life.

At ten o'clock that night the phone rang again. It was Roy, Roy Brown he now informed me. Yes, he had been at the service. He felt God had spoken to him. "I'll be all right now," he claimed. Still refusing to give his address, he agreed to meet me at two o'clock on Tuesday afternoon.

At five minutes to two that day the police called. "We have found the body of a man named Roy Brown in a gas-filled room at King's Cross," the sergeant said. "On him is a letter addressed to you."

"I am afraid my faith has failed me," said the letter. "Please pray for me. I am terribly afraid. Suicide is not the easy way out which many believe. The pressure of the past few weeks has been too much for me. A job and $300 would have saved me, but I just don't believe I'm worth it. I am a failure. I am leaving the world, unwanted, unloved, defeated, and without hope."

We could find no one who really cared for this thirty-eight-year-old Australian. Born an illegitimate child, he had known little of love. In debt, lonely, unemployed, he died his pitiable death.

So we buried him; the Central Methodist Mission paid for his funeral. My wife and I were the only persons present, and we had never even looked on his face.

I think I understand now a little more fully the aching heart of Jesus as he watched Judas rushing on to a suicide's end. How he must have yearned to save him. How he must have prayed that, like Peter, Judas would repent, confess his sins, and find a new life of hope. How wide and deep, had Judas but known it, was the love that followed him.

Jesus lost his man. But now the world knows that no one understands a suicide as Jesus does.

JESUS
AND A SEARCHER
AFTER TRUTH

On the great seal of Harvard
University is a single word *veritas*—"truth." It defines
the purpose of all education, the desire of all philosophy
and research, the aim of all schools and colleges—to
discover truth.

Across the story of Jesus is written the word "truth."
"Truth came through Jesus Christ," says John. Again,
"The Word became flesh and dwelt among us, full of

grace and truth." And Jesus himself claimed: "I am the way, and the truth and the life." Therefore the Christian faith and the whole intellectual quest for truth are tremendously mixed up together.

There are several occasions in the life of Jesus when he encountered somebody who was groping after the truth. Let us take one of them. It is the meeting between Jesus and Pilate. Jesus was brought to Pilate by the Jews for trial. Pilate, probing into his record, sought especially to discover whether he had any suspicious background. Presently he asked Jesus bluntly: "Are you a king, do you set yourself up as rival to Caesar?" Jesus said: "You say I am a king." He virtually argues in the words that follow that, yes, he is a king, but not a king who seeks by force to control men's bodies or their territories. He is a king of the realm of truth, of the minds and the souls of men. His power is exercised as his word is flashed from mind to mind and heart to heart in those that will be willing to receive it.

"Are you a king?" Yes, I am a king, Jesus admits, a king of this realm of truth. Hearing the word "truth" Pilate pounces on it and says, "What is truth?" Bacon in his essay *Of Truth* says: "What is truth? said jesting Pilate; and would not stay for an answer." I think Bacon was not at his penetrating best in such a comment. I can imagine Pilate often thinking quietly, as many a man would, of the meaning of life. Encountering somebody who he had heard was a great teacher he seriously, not in jest, asks his question. But after all,

81

there was not much opportunity for an answer. It was scarcely a time for philosophic inquiry.

What then is truth? What light does this encounter between Jesus and Pilate shed for us upon the search for truth?

Nobody in all history has so stimulated the search for truth as has Jesus Christ. Christ has shown in his own life that he was interested not only in feeling and action, He was interested in thought. Think for example of the tremendous intellectual insight of Jesus himself. We do not often talk about the intellectual power of Jesus, but was there ever anybody like him? If high intelligence expresses itself in being able to penetrate to the heart of an issue and to express that which is discovered succinctly, was there ever anyone to equal Jesus? He could sum up the commandments of the ages in a couple of sentences: "You shall love the Lord your God, . . . and your neighbor as yourself."

Who could give teachings by parables as Jesus did? No one has ever been his equal. What intellectual strength there is in the parables of the Prodigal Son or the Lost Sheep or the Good Samaritan! The most simple mind can grasp something of the meaning of the parables, but no one has ever been able to plumb their depth.

Think of the way in which Jesus has over all the centuries been ahead of, not behind, human progress. Surely one mark of a great mind is that it is far ahead of its period. Most religious teachers of history have stated views which have become a brake on progress. Look at the contrast between Jesus and Muhammad. Muhammad in his views regarding the relationships between men and women holds back the people's progress. Muhammad is responsible for keeping many women in bondage. Jesus, on the other hand, stands ahead of the conscience of humanity, calling mankind onward.

Out of the tremendous power of intellect of Jesus Christ has come the great intellectual heritage of Christianity. There have been few greater minds in all history than Saul of Tarsus who became Paul the Christian. Augustine, Luther, John Wesley, tower intellectually above the centuries. Today there appear no greater minds than Albert Schweitzer, William Temple, Paul Tillich, Reinhold Niebuhr, Emil Brunner, and Karl Barth.

Christ has encouraged the masses to seek for truth. It was not by accident that during the Dark Ages it was the Christian church which fiercely shielded the light of knowledge. It was not by accident that when an evangelical revival should come to England one of its first expressions should be in the Sunday schools of Robert Raikes. Sunday schools began with a two-fold purpose: to extend education and to bring children to God in Christ. It is not by accident that if you go to mission field after mission field today you find the church directing education. Before governments have found the energy or the resources to be there, the mission school has come into being, and more people are being led toward the light. There is no doubt about it: the Christian faith can afford to be judged by the way in which it has, over the centuries, stimulated the search for truth.

I have been recently reading the magnificent story of John Hunt, one of the first missionaries to reach Fiji. I think his life can almost be an illustration of the way Jesus stimulates the mind. John Hunt was just a plowboy in England. At sixteen years of age he was illiterate and ill schooled. Then he was converted in a Methodist meeting. Not only was his soul set on fire but his mind was set aflame. Eagerly he read the books a local Methodist preacher loaned him. Presently, inspired, he became the first Methodist minister in Great Britain to enter the new theological course that was established. Then this illiterate farm boy revealed astonishing, tremendous powers of the intellect. Quickly he learned Greek and Hebrew. On reaching Fiji as a missionary he mastered the Fijian language, giving to the Fijian people in a few short years the translation of the New Testament that has never been bettered.

What is truth? I am the truth, said Jesus. No one has stimulated the search for truth like Jesus.

Jesus Christ has set up the conditions whereby the search for truth can be advanced. There are people who sometimes claim that to become a Christian is to erect barriers against the free search after truth. To set up a point of reference in the first century, to accept doctrinal presuppositions, is to lose intellectual initiative and freedom.

Actually, the very reverse is true. Jesus Christ alone sets up the conditions through which full intellectual activity can proceed. Nicolas Berdyaev, the Russian Christian philosopher, points out it was Jesus Christ who established that there is one God, not many, and that God is not capricious but steadfast. This is, he claims, a prerequisite for responsible research and intellectual inquiry. If this world were a playground of multiple gods, or God could not be trusted to be consistent, research would be virtually impossible. In other words, it was Jesus Christ who set up the conditions in which research and modern science could develop. He established a world, a reliable world, where demons were subdued and where one God ruled. In this framework research and the whole development of modern intellectualism have become possible.

God is infinite mind. How can the search for truth be limited by a fact as vast as God? He is greater than the created universe. To think within the framework of his being is to operate in a larger arena than any bounded by matter and time. The really restricted thinker is the one who banishes God from all consideration, for he is stopping short of ultimate reality.

Jesus reminds us that a relevant fact in all inquiry and research is the quality of life of the one seeking truth. Jesus put it very bluntly once when he said: "The pure in heart shall see God."

Anatole France has a short story called "The Procurator of Judea." It discusses Pontius Pilate and Jesus. At one point Pontius Pilate is presented as an old man in retirement. A friend comes to see him, a friend who had been in Jerusalem when Pilate was there. Together they talk about an old love affair. Casually it is mentioned that the girl they are discussing became influenced by people called Christians. Then Pilate is asked whether he remembers Jesus. He puzzles for a moment and then says, "Jesus of Nazareth? No I cannot call him to mind."

Pilate in Jerusalem was near to the truth, yet he missed it. I wonder why. I believe it had something to do with the quality of Pilate's own life. Pilate was a man who had lost his integrity. His character was poor and weak. When the crowd shouted, "You are not Caesar's friend," he was prepared to put his own comfort and his own security before justice. Hence there developed one of the great miscarriages of justice in history. "The pure in heart shall see God." Pilate had no singleness of heart so he did not see God.

The personal equation cannot be canceled out in the search for truth. Even the scientist, dealing with precise and detailed facts, cannot forget who he is. The quality of a man's life has much to do with what he sees.

In the Old Testament the great assertion is made that bad men make false judgments. Evil seems to throw truth out of focus. Wickedness tampers with the processes of thought and influences the conclusions reached.

I can remember during the Second World War being seized with this claim of the Bible. Soon after, I happened to be sitting before a radio waiting for the four o'clock news to come from the British Broadcasting Corporation in London. Suddenly the voice announced that Hitler had invaded Russia. I can remember almost jumping to my feet and shouting: "Hitler you have committed your great blunder! Hitler, you are starting a war on two fronts! Hitler, this will be your undoing. Hitler, your wickedness has undermined your judgment!"

Again and again in history tyrants, evil men, have come to the moment when they have made a tragic and a disastrous intellectual choice. They have not seen clearly. Truth for them has become distorted. They have stumbled and fallen. The impure in heart and mind shall not see God, or be granted a vision of the truth.

The light of truth grows only as there is active commitment to it. As Alexander Miller puts it: "Truth-for-life is to be found in decision and identification, rather than in speculation."

Every student knows the tremendous power over the last fifty years of the school of thought known by the ugly name of existentialism. It claims that it is not in detachment from life but in involvement in it that understanding comes.

This is true. The important discoveries we make in so many areas of life escape us until we experience life in these areas ourselves. Until we love and suffer we know little about the meaning of love and suffering. Until we carry responsibility we see little of the affairs in which we may be immersed.

Here lay Pilate's error. He asked his question about truth, but it was given no follow-through. He gave no indication of being ready to act on any answer given to him. Therefore he missed the truth.

Truth-for-living cannot be found apart from active commitment to it. As John Baillie puts it: "Faith is apprehension through commitment." This is certainly true concerning discovering God in Jesus Christ. God is not found in detachment. There can be discussion, analysis, search, but the moment of commitment must come. God does not lie at the end of a logical argument. In the end there is no alternative to a leap of faith.

Leonard Griffith tells of a parachutist who learned of the thrill of trusting himself to what he believed was true. He described how he attended lectures about parachute jumping, learned the techniques, even jumped under simulated conditions. Then he said: "Nothing in this world compares with the thrill I experienced when I leaped into the sky, pulled the cord and found that the whole thing was actually true, that the parachute would support me and take me safely to the ground."

"Taste and see that the Lord is good" is the great invitation of the Bible. In picturesque language it is saying, "Put God to the test. Try him out. Begin to live as though there is a God, and you will find he is there."

Albert Schweitzer exercises a strange grip on the minds and hearts of men. His wisdom is listened to by millions. I wonder why. The chief reason is that he is more than a great philosopher, he is involved deeply in the human struggle. He is living what he sees. Hence men heed his words, follow his challenge.

Perhaps then we may be ready to find the truth as he has. His words are clear. At the end of his famous book *In Quest of the Historical Jesus* he puts it this way: "He comes to us as One unknown, without a name, as of old, by the lakeside. He came to those men who knew Him not. He speaks to us the same word: 'Follow thou me!' and sets us to the tasks which He has to fulfill for our time. He commands. And to those who obey Him, whether they be wise or simple, He will reveal Himself, . . . and they shall learn in their own experience Who He is."

"What is truth?" asked Pilate. "I am the way, and the truth and the life," is the answer Christ gives to us all.

JESUS
AND A PROSTITUTE

There is no more beautiful story in the Bible than the meeting between Jesus and the lonely, sinful woman of the city of Capernaum.

Jesus seems to have had friends in every section of society. In Capernaum there was a prominent Pharisee named Simon who invited him to dinner. For some reason his welcome to Jesus when he arrived was casual, if not discourteous. He supplied no water to wash the dust from his sandaled feet. There was no customary kiss of welcome. There was no anointing of head with oil or feet with ointment, as happened with any important guest.

The meal was eaten eastern fashion, with host and guests reclining on couches around a table. One strange custom was that people passing in the street would often enter the open house and watch what was happening. In other words a private function was also a public affair.

Therefore it was not unusual for a woman to step out of the darkness into the lighted banquet room of Simon's house. We watch her. For awhile she is scarcely noticeable as she presses against the wall.

Suddenly, impulsively, she moves. She comes to the feet of Jesus and draws a costly flask of ointment from the folds of her dress. As she prepares to pour it gently over his feet, tears well up in her eyes. She is greatly embarrassed as the tears fall on the feet of Jesus. Taking hold of the long tresses of her hair she quickly wipes away the tears.

By this time all present are very conscious of what is happening. Simon is shocked. He mutters to himself: "If this man were a prophet, he would have known who and what sort of woman this is who is touching him, for she is a sinner."

Then comes the rebuke. "Simon, I have something to say to you. Do you see this woman? When I entered your house you gave me no water for washing, no welcome kiss, no courteous anointing," said Jesus. With almost poetic rhythm he spells out Simon's neglect and the woman's love.

Turning to the woman standing silent, calmer now, no doubt wondering what is to happen, Jesus speaks his words of benediction. "Your sins are forgiven. Your faith has saved you; go in peace."

I am writing at a time when in a famous trial the women of another city who are sinners, women of London, move pathetically, brazenly across the pages of the newspapers. The story of Christ's forgiving and cleansing of the lonely woman of Capernaum seems to take on added meaning. Still amid the tumult of hot desire and public condemnation, how the word of redemption is needed: "Your sins are forgiven. Go in peace."

Jesus always drew lonely and sinful people to himself. Somewhere in Capernaum there lived this woman. When Jesus came to town, she knew it—he drew her like a magnet.

We know nothing of this woman of Capernaum except one thing, she was a "woman of the city," a prostitute. Somehow she had been drawn into one of the oldest forms of vice the world has known. But she was sick of it all, sick of herself, sick of sin.

What is the attitude of Jesus to sins of the flesh, to sensualism? Under no circumstances does he condone impurity. Indeed his probing glance penetrates far beyond the outward action. He looks on the heart and says: "He that looks at a woman lustfully has already

92

committed adultery with her in his heart." None has established a higher standard than he did.

Yet Jesus always showed deep understanding and sympathy with those who had fallen into sensual sin. To him bigotry of mind, intolerance, hatred of others, seemed more serious than the sin of impurity. Certainly his most searing words were reserved for the sins which came from closed minds and chilled hearts.

Today, however, a fight is joined between sexual license and Christian standards of purity and chastity. The truth is that Western sexual standards, never high, appear in these postwar years to have declined. Under the endless stimulation given by low-grade film and magazine producers—the "white slavers" of today's world—many have succumbed. If any reform is needed, it is for a purifying breeze to blow through the mass-media headquarters round the world. It is time to remember that sex standards and civilization rise and fall together.

In this crucial struggle Christian standards of sexual morality need reinterpreting. Sex, to the Christian, is a great and glorious gift of God, too great to be marred by seamy unions outside the marriage bond. It is not evil in itself, for God made it.

Chastity, as J. A. T. Robinson has pointed out, is right because it is the expression of caring, of caring enough. Fornication is wrong because it is a denial of love. However, in the wider companionship of marriage all lingering ideas of guilt should go from physical union. Christian morality boldly, gladly endorses scientific birth control because, for the first time, it permits unclouded creative joy in the marriage bond.

In the attitude of Jesus to the woman of the city of Capernaum we see his call to all who have fallen below his standards of inner and outer purity. It is a call to repentance.

An unresolved discussion, even after all these years, centers on the incident in Simon's house. It is a discussion as to what led the woman to break her costly flask of ointment over the feet of Jesus. Was it an act of gratitude or repentance?

The woman could have met Jesus before. As with the woman taken in adultery and brought before Jesus, he somewhere else could have brought peace to her divided life. Now, as he comes to Capernaum again, she has a chance to show her love and gratitude for all he has done. The tears then become tears of joy, the ointment is an offering of thanksgiving.

Some facts point to this interpretation. Jesus himself told a story to Simon, a story of forgiveness. He said there were once two men who owed money. One owed five hundred denarii and one owed fifty denarii. A denarius was the most common Roman coin. It was valued at about twenty cents and was a laborer's pay for a day. Both had their debts canceled. "Which would love the creditor most?" asked Jesus. "The one, I suppose, to whom he forgave more," replied Simon. "Right," said

Jesus, and turned to offer his generous forgiveness to the woman.

This story Jesus told seems to suggest the flask of ointment was a flask of gratitude. Also, the fact that the woman had the ointment all ready for use points to this interpretation.

Yet I wonder. There are other facts which point to the other conclusion. There are the signs of penitence. The tears of the woman could have been tears of penitence. Jesus certainly seems to treat her as an unforgiven sinner. It would not be like him to deal with the same sins twice. For him forgiveness meant God's forgetfulness of sin forever.

I believe, then, that the story of the woman at Capernaum is a story of confession and forgiveness. The coming of the woman was the search of a stained, sinful life for pardon. Gloriously, forgiveness was received.

There is a wonderful story in the writings of George Macdonald about another woman who was a sinner. The scene is set in a house of ill fame. One of the women was desperately ill. To the house came a man named Falconer who tried to bring comfort. Let the rest be told in George Macdonald's own words.

Falconer sat down on the side of the bed and read the story of Simon the Pharisee and the woman that was a sinner. When he ceased the silence that followed was broken by a sob from somewhere in the room. The sick woman said: "Turn down the leaf, there please sir. Lilywhite will read it to me when you're gone."

The same one sobbed again. It was a young slender girl. Falconer said something gentle to her.

"Will He ever come again?" she asked.

"Who?"

"Him—Jesus Christ. I've heard tell, I think, that he was to come again some day."

"Why do you ask?"

"Because—" she said, with a fresh burst of tears, which rendered the words that followed unintelligible. But she recovered herself in a few minutes and, as if finishing her sentence, put her hand up to her poor thin, colourless hair and said: "My hair ain't long enough to wipe His feet."

One fact stands out very clearly in the story of the nameless woman at Capernaum. It is that Jesus saw her not as she was, but as she might become.

"Do you see this woman?" said Jesus to Simon. It is so simple a question. Yet what depths there are in it.

Simon did not see the woman, not really. To him she was a type, a harlot. That summed her up. She was placed in her category, and that was the end of it. There was no understanding of her needs and aspirations. There was no seeing her as a person.

From seeing people as types rather than persons comes the ugly spirit of moral judgment which so often crushes human yearnings for goodness. Nothing sends people reeling back into their sin more quickly than moral condemnation.

Often in the New Testament Jesus is seen breaking from the moral judgments of self-righteous people to stand beside the one being judged. With an outcast like

Zacchaeus, a woman taken in adultery, and here with a sinner in Simon's house, he reaches out a hand to someone under judgment and draws that one toward salvation.

Jesus sees us as we really are. What a comfort there is in this fact for most of us. He looks upon us, not only as we are but as we might become, by his grace. In this fact is our hope and our salvation.

The climax of the story is the fact of forgiveness. There is heard in that ancient dining room the wonderful words: "Your sins are forgiven, go in peace."

Paul Tournier, the Swiss psychiatrist, claims there are two kinds of guilt. "False guilt," he says, "is that which comes as a result of the judgments and suggestions of men. True guilt is that which results from Divine judgment."

There is certainly a deep mystery about the nature of guilt. There are some acts which place a burden, a terrible burden, on the human heart. We know of some of them. Murder involves deep guilt. Adultery creates deep guilt. Dishonesty leads to deep guilt. Cruelty means deep guilt.

When true guilt is involved, only God can act. If guilt rises from a breaking of God's law, from an alienation from God's presence, only God can remove it. He alone can speak the words: "Your sins are forgiven."

The amazing, glorious fact of the Christian gospel is that God in Christ Jesus has spoken that word. To sinner after sinner in the New Testament he brought certainty of pardon. Today, with his death on the cross confirming it all, we know the miracle of forgiveness is a fact. To us he speaks the word—forgiveness.

During 1963 in Australia a remarkable book was published. It is the story of a man named John Knatchbull, who was sent from England to Australia in 1824 as a convict. After incredible experiences of cruelty and suffering he was finally executed for murder before ten thousand people at Darlinghurst in Sydney in 1844.

As he lay awaiting execution John Knatchbull wrote his life story. Only now, after all these years, has the manuscript been discovered. It has allowed a new estimate of the life and condemnation of one who was a notorious criminal in Australia's early history. John Knatchbull, it now appears, was falsely and savagely sentenced to transportation to Australia at the instigation of a relative. In Sydney he was forced to endure the suffering and cruelty of those bitter days. He was sent even farther, to Norfolk Island, which was the penalty given to convicts who were sentenced for further acts of defiance at the convict colony of Sydney.

On return to Sydney the injustice and cruelty he had suffered welled up, leading him to commit a ruthless murder—perhaps the one act of his life for which he was really guilty. It was for this crime he was publicly hanged.

It was during his final trial and the days when he was

awaiting death that the John Knatchbull story became a wonderful story of redemption.

A Christian woman, a Mrs. Latham, attended John Knatchbull's trial. As he was taken back to his cell she seized the opportunity for which she had planned. She was able to say quietly and sincerely to him: "Make your peace with Almighty God."

Back in his cell John Knatchbull could not get the kindness of the woman's face or her genuine, intense words out of his mind. It was almost the first tender act he had received for years.

He sent for Mrs. Latham. She came, together with the minister of the Pitt Street Congregational Church in Sydney. They talked to him of the love and the forgiveness of God.

Then it happened. Pardon, salvation broke into the heart of the condemned man. "No tongue can express my feelings until I flew to prayer and meditated on the advice given me by Mrs. Latham: 'make your peace with God.' Now I received the full force of her benevolent intention.

"Now would I have given the treasures of the East had I seen her years ago: what a different man should I have been."

In this faith John Knatchbull died. He spent the night before his execution in prayer. He went calmly to the scaffold in the power of the faith which had come to him. "By putting my trust in Christ," he wrote,

99

"laying all my past sins at the foot of the Cross, Christ would in no wise cast me out."

So another joined the fellowship of the forgiven. He heard the words the woman at Capernaum discovered. They are the words you can receive too: "Your sins are forgiven. Go in peace."

JESUS
AND THE MAN WHO
WANTED TO PRAY

No man ever prayed as Jesus did. After two thousand years we can still sense in the pages of the New Testament the tremendous impact the praying Christ made on his contemporaries. Jesus inaugurated a new era in personal, intimate prayer. He moved the world by prayer.

No wonder one of the disciples came to Jesus and said simply, "Lord, teach us to pray." There is no indication where this incident occurred. We can imagine the scene. Jesus had drawn aside from the crowd, then from his actual friends. Perhaps they could see him or even hear him as he began to pray. It was apparently his practice to pray aloud. As he prayed God seemed very near, for indeed he was.

Presently Jesus returned with his face shining from the intimacy and the joy of his fellowship with God. Beside it all the prayer of the disciples appeared so unreal, so shallow, so proverty-stricken.

The world owes a tremendous debt of gratitude to the unnamed disciple who perhaps voiced the yearning of many and wanted to know how to pray. It brought from Jesus the priceless gift of the Lord's Prayer, which now millions of people pray every day.

"Lord, teach us to pray." Modern man needs this help from Jesus, too. Recently in a large American church a minister asked members of his congregation to list the subjects on which they would most like him to preach. At the top of the list was the request to give guidance on how to pray.

Prayer is probably the most believed in, least practiced activity in the world. Probably most people pray in some kind of way sometimes, especially in a crisis. However, regular, real prayer is rare.

Some time ago I made a survey of the religious attitudes and habits of people in an Australian town. It appeared that among Protestants the old practice of "family prayers" had virtually disappeared. Among

Roman Catholics the saying of the Rosary showed a similar decline. Even the simple act of grace before meals had died out in all but fifteen of every one hundred homes. In the upper grades in the high school only a few girls and fewer boys prayed before going to bed at night or at any other time.

Many explanations may be given as to why people, most of whom claim to believe in God, fail to pray. One reason is ignorance as to how effectively to enter into the difficult practice of prayer. Still the cry rises: "Lord, teach us to pray."

A. J. Gossip in his book on prayer has one chapter entitled "On Thinking Magnificently About God." This is where prayer must always begin—in holding aloft the greatness of God.

If we study the prayers of Jesus we find that he always began by thinking magnificently about God, his Heavenly Father. Think of the reply he gave to the disciple who wanted to pray. When you pray, say,

> Our Father who art in heaven,
> Hallowed be thy name.
> Thy Kingdom come,
> Thy will be done,
> On earth as it is in heaven.

See where he starts. It is not with man, not with human need, not with the cry of the despairing spirit, but with God. The hallowed wonder of God, the glory of his kingdom, the reality of his will are first emphasized. Prayer must always begin with God.

There are obviously two ways of approaching God. One is from our side, as it were. We commence with the yearning of our spirits, we pour out our sorrows, our troubles. Then we try to think of his coming into our human situation. We sincerely attempt to place all that has happened to us in the context of his love and purpose. In other words we begin with ourselves and move on and up to God.

There is a serious danger in this approach. It is that we get caught in the morass of our own anxieties and sins, our own doubts and emotions. By going over and over again in the presence of God our own problems and difficulties, we can merely push them deeper into our consciousness. Then we can rise from our knees literally worse than when we bowed to pray.

There is another way of praying. It is to start at God's side and from there move downward into our personal and corporate situation. We establish a frame of reference for our affairs before we concentrate our thought on our need.

Jesus said, "When you pray, say: 'Our Father who art in heaven.'" There is no doubt about the way Jesus prayed. He began with God. Then he came to voicing the need for bread and forgiveness and for finding a power to overcome evil.

I can only confess that many times I have discovered the power of prayer when I have prayed this way. Depressed, frightened, I have forced my mind to dwell on some attribute of God. Merely to think of God has seemed to break the mesmeric power of my own pre-occupations with my own mood. Then the magnetism of God has begun to operate and I have been drawn upward to sanity and wholeness.

Few men have revealed greater power in prayer than John Hunt, the saintly missionary to Fiji. When a student at theological college in England, John Hunt established his habits in prayer which he followed for the rest of his life.

John Hunt gave the first hour of each day to prayer. His first act was to look toward God. He would praise him for his goodness, for his care over the night that had passed, for the providence which encircled Hunt's life.

Next he would quietly and thoughtfully repeat the Lord's Prayer. Now he would be ready to raise his own needs and concerns. He would move, one by one, through the known tasks of the coming day, seeking wisdom and strength for each of them. He would ask for the baptism of the Holy Spirit for all he had to do.

After a period when he would devotionally read his Bible, he would move on to intercession. He would mention the members of his family, the circle of his friends, and his companions in his missionary labors, naming them one by one before God. The hour would by this time be nearly gone, but he would take time to intercede for the church and the world.

There is the sequence we all should follow. It was the method of one greater than John Hunt. Begin with God, thinking magnificently about God.

"Lord, teach us to pray." Jesus teaches us to pray confidently and expectantly. Always, when we pray we should expect things to happen.

The whole of the life of Jesus is an illustration of believing prayer. Jesus often seemed to thank God for something before it happened.

Take for example the story of Lazarus. Jesus came to the tomb where Lazarus lay dead and buried. Before the grave was opened Jesus said simply: "I thank thee that thou hast heard me." Jesus prayed believingly.

There are few places where the ideas of a scientific age have seeped further than in relation to prayer. We carry a mental picture of a world governed by natural law, a cast-iron universe where only cause and effect operate. Even as we pray, this idea of the world intrudes, ruling out the possibility of any free act of God.

If we would only stop and analyze the assumptions which lie behind this view of God and his world, we would see how limited they are. Spontaneity, no less than rigid obedience to law, can be seen in the universe and in history.

A suggestive definition of a miracle says that it is an event with which human comprehension has not yet caught up. It is not an interruption of law, but the working of a law which human reason has not yet chartered.

Here is a further reason why we can pray with confidence. By praying, as for the sick in mind or body, we may be tapping resources we cannot grasp and allowing God to bring into operation his higher laws.

Often when God has creatively and positively been at work, we express our ignorance, perhaps our unbelief, by saying, "It happened." What happened, and why? What brought that unexpected combination of circumstances into play?

A strange series of happenings occurred here in Sydney which some may call coincidence, but which I am convinced was the wonderful working of the Spirit of God.

It began with a telephone call. A woman called me and said that she had a large home on an acre of ground which had become too much for her to maintain. She thought it might be used as a home for children, and she offered it at a much reduced price. I thanked her but doubted if anything could be done as we had other costly projects on hand.

Some weeks later I visited a Sydney businessman to seek financial help for a youth center we were building. "I will help in a small way," he said. Then he added, "Someday I would like to choose one area of need and give substantially to it. I have always been interested in children." The comment registered, but that was all.

Again weeks passed, until at a meeting of the executive board of our existing children's home we were told

107

we were turning away fifty children a week and that need was outstripping all the facilities of the city. Facing the situation we prayed God might show us what to do.

That night my wife remembered the offered home, and I remembered the businessman's comment. To our delight we found the home was still available. A visit to the businessman resulted in his agreeing to see it. I dared to say, "I wonder, would you consider buying it, and giving it to us as a second home for needy and deserted children?"

Two days later the home was ours. And that is how the Bernard-Smith Children's Home in Sydney came into existence.

Coincidence or God? For me there is only one answer. God was far more concerned about the need of unwanted and helpless children than we were. Prayer and concern allowed him to act. His Spirit dropped an idea here, made a suggestion there. His pattern of events emerged. Prayer was answered. It is the kind of happening which should encourage us to pray believingly.

"Lord, teach us to pray." Jesus calls us to pray persistently. It is determined, costly prayer which enables the grace of God to come flooding down into the human situation.

Jesus once told a little story which comes straight out of the East. The poorer people of Palestine and India with no adequate lighting in their homes go to bed at the same time as the roosters. Also in the small, one-room houses parents are forced to sleep with their children.

Jesus described how a man came to a friend's house in a certain village after dark to ask for hospitality. Again there is a glimpse of the poverty surrounding the life of those far-off days. There was no food in the house.

Hurrying to another house the villager seeks food for his friend. When he knocks, a sleepy voice asks from within what he wants. On hearing the request for food the sleepy man shows no enthusiasm to help. "I'm in bed with my children," he says. Apparently there is bread, but he does not want to have to rise and give it. And so he turns over and tries to go back to sleep. But the knocking is determined. At last, perhaps knowing his neighbor is one not easily put off, to get peace and sleep he rises and gives the bread. Determined asking brought results.

Always in the stories Jesus told he was seeking to convey one central truth. Here he is declaring that prayer must be persistent.

When we come to think of it, much of our prayer is casual and spasmodic. We almost skip up to God, present a request or two, and scarcely giving him time to answer, we are gone. And we claim to be surprised when nothing happens.

Compare this kind of praying with an incident from

109

the life of William Temple. He once had a difficult decision to make. At eight o'clock one evening he began to pray, centering his mind and all his resources on coming to know God's will. For three hours he prayed, intensely, with singleness of purpose. At eleven o'clock, he said: "I knew perfectly well what I had got to do."

There is a costly identification necessary with the ones for whom we pray if our intercessions are to possess power with God. By thinking deeply into the situation of the ones in need, by standing where they stand, we make it possible for God to work through us.

A friend is sick and we dare to pray for him. What is involved? We think of his circumstances, we try to imagine his anxieties. The sickness has struck suddenly, a mysterious pain pointing to some deep-seated trouble. Of course, he thinks it could be cancer. There is dread, tremendous dread as the day of the operation comes near—dread of what may be found. Financial anxieties are there. How will he pay those bills? Modern hospital costs reach almost astronomical proportions. If his meager savings are used up, how will he and his family face a long convalescence? And what of his wife, looking on with fear? What are her needs at this hour?

So with intense identification prayer proceeds. With love, the true love of a neighbor and a friend, welling up all is carried before God in prayer.

Do you and I pray like this? Having prayed once

do we go on praying? Do we, as Jacob who wrestled with the angel at Peniel until dawn, say, "I will not cease until the Lord blesses my friend." It is this costly, persistent praying which enables God to answer.

"Lord, teach us to pray." Prayer, as Jesus defined it, is not only word speaking, it is a life-giving act. It is prayer which, beginning with God and moving through costly identification with the purposes of God and the needs of those for whom we pray, becomes self-dedication.

Never shall I forget the night before Good Friday which I spent in the Garden of Gethsemane. In the evening I set off from Jerusalem, across the brook Kidron, up the slopes of Olivet, until there I was at the entrance to the garden.

Pressing on through the gnarled olive trees, I came to a quiet place where perhaps Jesus had said to his men, "Sit here, while I go yonder and pray." As I knelt it was not difficult to imagine Jesus on that night long ago. I could almost see his bowed figure. The soft night seemed filled with voices. I seemed to hear the intensity of a man praying. As I repeated in my mind the words of his prayer, the climax was nearly unbearable. "Father, if thou art willing, remove this cup from me; nevertheless not my will, but thine, be done."

Because to Jesus prayer involved an intensely personal and intimate relationship with God, he could offer nothing less than his whole being to God. He recognized

111

that many times we can become the instruments in God's hands through which he can answer the prayers we have uttered.

We still cling to many ideas which belonged to the old mechanical prayer wheel. We falsely think the power lies in the prayer, not with God, the object of prayer. Therefore we imagine that if we repeat enough prayer phrases often enough, the answer will come.

I recall an incident which shocked me. It occurred in my first Australian church, at a place called Cessnock. It was early in the Second World War, and the king had called for a national day of prayer. On my way to church that Sunday morning, I met a prominent businessman of the town, heading toward worship. His reputation was not exactly a savory one, and to my knowledge he had not been seen inside a church for years.

"I'm coming to your church today," he said. "I'd better do my bit for the empire and send up a prayer." I thought his words just about blasphemy.

Compare such an attitude with that of Florence Nightingale. There settled on her heart and conscience the suffering and degradation of the soldiers engaged in the Crimean War. She prayed for them. Then out of her prayer emerged a high resolve.

"O God," she prayed, "O God that fillest my heart with this great desire to devote myself to the sick and the sorrowful, I offer my heart to Thee, I offer my heart to Thee."

Prayer cannot stop short of a deep act of self-giving. "I offer my heart to thee" is the cry of Florence Nightingale. "Thy will be done," said Jesus as he moved from the prayer of Gethsemane to the sacrifice of Calvary.

"Lord, teach us to pray."

JESUS
AND A MAN
PARALYZED BY SIN

Sin is sadder than sorrow. Sin stops at nothing. It robs a man of inner integrity and self-respect. It destroys human relationships, dividing friends and families. It corrupts society, working itself out in conflict and war. Sin separates man from God, making him feel a lonely orphan in a condemning universe.

There is a story told in three of the Gospels—Matthew, Mark, and Luke—which shows the power of sin to paralyze the body. One day a group of friends decided to bring a young man who was paralyzed to Jesus. He could have been just a teen-age boy, for Jesus later used a word in addressing him which means "lad."

When they reached the house where Jesus was staying, they found such a crowd around the door there was no chance of pushing their way to his side. So, climbing up on the flat-roofed house—a typical Palestine home—they pulled aside the roof slabs and lowered the boy on a stretcher in front of Jesus.

"My son, your sins are forgiven," were the first words of Jesus. Surprise spread across the many faces. Some wondered what the mention of sins had to do with one brought for physical healing. Others found the claim to be able to forgive sins objectionable in the light of their religious convictions.

Jesus sensed what was being thought and whispered, "Why do you question thus in your hearts?" Then Jesus asserted it was harder to forgive sin than to restore a paralyzed man. To prove his authority in forgiveness he said to the helpless man, "Rise, . . . and walk." And he did, and hurried to his home, carrying the stretcher on which he had been brought, to tell the wonderful news of his healing to his family.

There is a tremendously important truth hidden in this simple and moving story. It is the truth that spirit and flesh are closely linked, that sometimes the ills of the body have their root in mind and emotion. The claim emerges that healing of spirit brings about the restoration of strength to the body.

Jesus brought healing to the paralyzed man because he saw the man's personality in its wholeness. By seeing men and women in body, mind, and spirit, he was able to penetrate behind symptoms to causes, to send healing power flooding through every corner of personality.

In this area of healing modern medicine only now seems to be catching up with the insight of Jesus. There has been much treatment of the body without recognition of its relation to the spirit. As a result sometimes the body has been healed leaving the maladjusted spirit to begin at once again to produce the same bodily disharmony.

One of the thrilling developments in recent years has been the coming closer together of religion and medical science of minister and doctor. The judgment of a medical specialist in Sydney, R. L. Walker, would be increasingly accepted. At a conference of clergy and doctors he said: "A satisfactory state of mental function as regards intellect, emotion, and instinct is as vital to health as is the normal pulse of the heart."

Evidence is mounting of the vast extent of sickness which has its root in mind and spirit. The medical superintendent of a large London hospital recently claimed that fifty per cent of patients reveal that the origin of their disease is in the mind. Anxiety, worry, guilt, resentment, undisciplined ambition, unhappy relationships between husband and wife, all take it out on the body.

The derivation of the word "health" gives a clue as to its true nature. It comes from an old English word "hale," which meant something similar to our word holiness. In other words the relationship of a man or a woman with God has much to do with health. Holiness of life can mean health.

Jesus, peering into the life of the young man brought to him for healing, saw that unforgiven sin was causing the paralysis of limb. A sense of guilt lay behind the helplessness of his body.

The world, since the Second World War, has been in a chastened mood. Mankind imagined it had moved beyond some of the evils of history. Then came the concentration camps and the gas ovens of Nazi Germany. Hiroshima, in one dreadful act of man's inhumanity to man, perished in a sea of flame.

Since then nothing has happened to reassure man that he is successfully leaving evil behind. The bloodshed of Hungary and Suez, the execution squads of Castro's Cuba, have shocked the world. Then followed the evils of the year 1963, the Profumo scandal of Great Britain and that terrible expression of hatred and extremism which destroyed President Kennedy. Before all such evidence only the very foolish can make light of evil.

Sin is destroying many individual lives. Guilt, the consequence of sin, is playing havoc with personal well-

117

being. As Donald Baillie rightly says: "A great many persons in the world today have something like a repressed moral-failure complex. They do not confess their sins to God or man, but they have an uneasy dissatisfaction with themselves and with what they have made of their moral opportunity."

Guilt always possesses the power to shatter personality. George McLeod says that nearly half the hospital beds occupied in Great Britain on any day of the year are occupied by mental cases. Of these, half are there because of an overloaded sense of guilt. The superintendent of an asylum said recently he could release half of his patients if someone could assure them that their guilt would be taken away.

Guilt paralyzes the body. There are many modern counterparts to the stricken man brought to Jesus. By the pronouncement of the word "forgiveness, by the removal of the crippling sense of guilt, he was made whole. Perhaps some men and women, lying helplessly in bed, sitting imprisoned in a wheelchair, would rise up and walk if only, only the forgiveness of God could be believed and accepted.

Guilt paralyzes the human spirit. Joy and guilt cannot exist together. Guilt destroys creativity, so clouding the sky that there is little mood to fashion something new. Guilt removes God from our side, and without God life becomes scarcely worth living.

Guilt paralyzes marriage. I have been staggered over recent years at the power of guilt rising from mishandled sex life before and after marriage. I have seen homes breaking down because years later guilt for premarital unchastity lingers. I have grappled with the problems of adultery and abortion and their effect on the continuing relationships between a husband and a wife. Without forgiveness from God and then from each other, there was no hope. With the acceptance of forgiveness a great load was lifted and the paralysis of a marriage passed.

Let me choose one illustration which will not involve the breaking of a confidence, for permission has been given for the story to be told. There came to my office a young married woman, obviously on the edge of a mental and emotional breakdown. Happily married until six months before she was now "unable to understand herself." Tension and conflict had developed in the home. She wondered whether she loved her husband, or even her two children. Weeping constantly, she knew she was no companion for any man, no fit mother for any children.

At last, after two sessions of groping for causes, the seat of the trouble was reached. She blurted out the story of the conceiving of a third child, of her conviction that under inflationary conditions in Australia they could not afford a third baby. There followed the furtive operation, the loss of the child, and the seemingly quick recovery.

Now, after three years, the guilt had grown in intensity until, though unconscious, it was destroying her home. I shall not forget the sense of deliverance which came to her when I was able to say, in the name of Jesus, "Your sins are forgiven."

There was a sequel. Her husband was shortly after transferred to another state. At their request I used for them a simple rededication marriage service. In Wesley Chapel, two people, their marriage made whole again, joyfully renewed their vows to each other and to God. I witnessed the ancient miracle, with its sequence of first forgiveness, then healing. And Jesus said: "Your sins are forgiven. Rise up, . . . and walk!"

How do we move from hearing the voice of conscience to receiving the word of forgiveness? How do we reach the point where, having confessed our sin, we "accept our acceptance," to use Paul Tillich's notable phrase? How do we become certain of the pardon of God?

Jesus was able to help the paralyzed man, from guilt through forgiveness to healing, because he was able with authority to prounounce those words: "Your sins are forgiven." This is the secret of the story, the power of Jesus to bring about the miracle of forgiveness.

Man cannot forgive himself. No matter how often he tells himself that his sin was not serious, it remains to haunt him. Some word from beyond must come if he is to find peace of heart, the only peace there is.

Man's inability to forgive himself is demonstrated in the strange novel by Albert Camus called *The Fall*. The central character in the story is a Parisian lawyer, self-assured, respected, secure in his self-esteem. Then one night, walking home late across a bridge over the Seine, something happens which he was never able to forget. It was his "fall."

"I had already gone some fifty yards" he said, "when I heard the sound of a body striking the water. I heard a cry, repeated several times which was going downstream; then it suddenly ceased. I wanted to run and yet didn't stir. Then slowly under the rain I went away. I informed no one. The next day and the days following, I didn't read the papers."

Always thereafter the memory of that incident haunted him. Years later, still bearing his inner sense of guilt he said: "O young woman, throw yourself in the water again so that I may a second time have the chance of saving both of us. It's too late now, it will always be too late."

We cannot speak the word "forgiveness" to one another and erase the deep guilt which we know has involved us with God. More and more of us are rushing to psychiatrists, hoping they with their techniques may deliver us.

But it is more than a question of techniques. It is the word, the living, liberating word, which human techniques may convey to us. A psychiatrist may uncover the hidden fears, the deep-seated motive, the lurking guilt. What then? God must speak or there is silence.

David Stafford-Clark, a Christian psychiatrist, poses the dilemma and points to the answer. In his book *Psy-*

121

chiatry To-day he writes: "Thrown back upon himself the patient finds no solace, no comfort. He looks to his psychiatrist. He cannot get power from him. If he could it would not be maintained for life."

Then Dr. Clark adds: "Where then can a man turn? As a psychiatrist I know of no answer to this question: as a man I can only say with all humility, I believe in God."

Horatius Bonar has the answer in one of his poems. Listen to it.

> Not what these hands have done
>   Can save this guilty soul;
> Not what this toiling flesh has borne
>   Can make my spirit whole.
> Thy love to me, O God
>   Not mine, O Lord, to Thee,
> Can rid me of this dark unrest,
>   And set my spirit free.

There is only one place in all the world where we become absolutely convinced our sins can be and are forgiven. It is in the presence of Jesus. The world of nature carries no conviction. To stand at night under a starry sky looking heavenward may speak to us of God as Creator, but the world of nature speaks no word of forgiveness. History with its strange twistings and turnings bears witness to the judgments of God. History is the story of the judgments of God. But the voice of history is not the voice of forgiveness. Our own conscience condemns, but it can never speak forgiveness.

Jesus speaks this word. He carries conviction. In the days of his flesh he made people believe he had power to forgive sins. Adulterers believed him, extortioners believed him, the paralyzed man believed him, his disciples believed him, his enemies believed him.

Today you and I can believe him. The risen Christ with authority says to you and to me: "Your sins are forgiven."

There is one other sentence in the story of the man who was paralyzed by sin which we must not miss. It is the comment of the Gospels: "When Jesus saw their faith, he said to the paralytic, 'My son, your sins are forgiven.'"

What a picture of the faithful solicitude of friends is given in the story. Four friends brought the paralyzed one to Jesus. They were determined. They even climbed on the roof, and, with real ingenuity, lowered him to the very feet of Jesus. Great must have been their faith, for Jesus saw it and Jesus honored it. Their faith played a large part in the forgiveness and the healing which flowed.

Do we believe enough to bring our friends to Jesus for the touch of his power? Do we? How long has it been since we prayed for that sick member of the family circle, that friend? How long has it been since we tried to bring someone whom we know to church, believing perhaps a word will be heard there which will bring

123

about deliverance? How determined are we? Have we ever done anything as persistently and imaginatively as the four who climbed a rooftop for a friend's sake?

The atmosphere which surrounds a patient in an operating theater is to the surgeon all important. Every effort is made by sterilization of instruments, by cleanliness, by protective action by the hospital staff, to provide the right, germ-free atmosphere for healing.

Does prayer create an atmosphere in which God can work? I suggest this is just what it does. Prayer gives to a friend who is desperately sick a better chance of recovery than one whose life is not so encompassed. On the stretcher of prayer we may bring a friend to Jesus.

"And when Jesus saw their faith he said, . . . 'your sins are forgiven.'" Saw their faith! Intercessory prayer possesses power. Faith on behalf of another brings results. Saw their faith!

The Danish theologian Sören Kierkegaard gives a definition of what the Christian faith really is. "The Christian religion is this: the profound humiliation of man, the boundless love of God, the endless striving born of gratitude."

In gratitude for what God has done for us, we bring our friends to Jesus. We bring them in faith. Forgiveness may come to them, healing may follow. Seeing our faith Christ may free our friends from guilt, free them for service. This is our privilege. We may help Jesus to help our friends.

JESUS
AND THE HONEST
DOUBTER

Neither doubt nor sin blocks
our coming to God. Jesus treats with understanding our
intellectual imperfections as he does our moral failures.
He forgives the incompleteness of our faith as he does
our behavior and our sin.

The way Jesus deals with the honest doubter is seen
in the story of Thomas, one of the twelve disciples.
Thomas is one of the lesser known followers of Jesus.
His name appears halfway in the list of disciples,

which perhaps shows his relative importance among the twelve. All we actually know of him is found in the 155 words with which his story is recorded in the Gospel of John.

We first see Thomas as a man of courage. News has come that Lazarus is sick. Jesus at once announces that he is going to his side, which means a journey to Judea. The disciples protest, for they know the peril Jesus will face as he enters the area of Jerusalem where his enemies are so strong. They say, "Rabbi, the Jews were but now seeking to stone you, and are you going there again?" Thomas rallies the wavering disciples by saying simply: "Let us also go, that we may die with him."

Thomas next steps out of obscurity in the Upper Room. There the questing mind, the somewhat bewildered spirit appear. Jesus has spoken of leaving his men, but tells them that they will know where he will be and there will join him.

Bluntly Thomas speaks: "Lord, we do not know where you are going, how can we know the way?" This query brought from Jesus the sublime answer: "I am the way, and the truth, and the life."

Once more we meet Thomas. It is after the resurrection when doubt dominates his mind, but doubt which finally comes through to blazing faith.

Thomas is not with the other disciples when Jesus appears among them. On hearing their testimony he says: "Unless I see in his hands the print of the nails and place my finger in the mark of the nails, and place my hand in his side, I will not believe."

Days later, as though Jesus had heard the earlier conversation—as indeed he had in his risen power—he suddenly appeared at Thomas' side. Jesus said to Thomas, "Put your finger here, and see my hands; and put out your hand, and place it in my side; do not be faithless, but believing."

Then comes the greatest declaration of faith in all the New Testament: "My Lord and my God!" The doubter has at last found certainty.

Through these brief incidents we see a character of great attractiveness drawn for us. Thomas is a man whose mind is cast in a modern mold; he asks probing questions, he demands satisfying answers.

James Hastings gives a thumbnail character sketch of the man. "Thomas is incredulous but tenacious, despondent but true, little hope but much courage, sincere in love though perplexed in faith, neither rushing to right conclusions like Peter, nor rushing away from them into danger and dishonour as Peter did."

What is more important, we see in the story of Thomas the way Jesus tries to help a man with a somewhat different kind of problem from most he faced—the problem of doubt. We see him tenderly, patiently leading Thomas from sincere doubt to full faith.

Jesus called Thomas to be with him. We have no record of how or where Jesus said to Thomas, "Follow me." But choose him he did, selecting him to be one of those immortal twelve who would become "fishers of men."

I am glad there was one among the early disciples who had an inquiring, even a skeptical, mind. Even before the scientific era he wanted proof for what he accepted and believed. Thomas stands nearer the modern intellectual mood than any of the other disciples.

There are some Christian groups which go much further than their Master in demanding doctrinal purity at every point and intellectual subservience to creedal statements. Perhaps some of us need to admit that Jesus always respects what Herbert Farmer calls "the sacred right of rejection," which resides in human personality. The presence of Thomas in the list of the twelve disciples guarantees the intellectual integrity which Jesus expects of all who follow him.

Jesus has always been able to enlist men and women of strong and independent minds in his cause. No Christian mind in the ancient world was greater than Paul. He was an early representative of a long line of people with notable intellects who have been proud to bow before Jesus. We can name some of them: Augustine, Abelard, Thomas Aquinas, Calvin, Martin Luther, John Wesley. Nor has the line become exhausted. Today's world has few if any to compare with William Temple, Karl Barth, Emil Brunner, Reinhold Niebuhr, Albert Schweitzer in quality of mind.

The important fact to remember is that Christ accepts us with our doubts and with our unresolved intellectual difficulties. He asks only that we offer him our allegiance, setting out on the road with him, waiting for the light to grow. For after all, to be a Christian is to be loyal not to a set of intellectual propositions but to a person named Jesus.

Jesus, when he set out for Judea because Lazarus was sick, gratefully accepted the courage of Thomas. In the first glimpse we have of the character of Thomas he emerges as a brave man committed completely to his Lord.

I suggest that at this time there were doubts and unanswered questions in the mind of Thomas, but there were also the truths in which he did believe, and above all the Christ whom he loved. So giving himself utterly to the truth which he could accept, he was ready even to die for it.

Dorothy Sayers in her series of plays on the life of Jesus called *The Man Born to Be King* has caught the mood of Thomas. When Jesus announces he is going to Judea the disciples shrink back in alarm from the dangers of the journey.

Peter says: "That's a fact. We've got to trust him to know what's right. And after all, he came out safe before." Thomas replies: "I shouldn't count on that. What I say is, he's our Master and our friend; and if he's going to be killed, let us go too, and die with him." [1]

The American theologian Horace Bushnell when at

[1] From *The Man Born to Be King* (New York: Harper & Row Inc., 1949), "The Light and the Life," Scene III, page 189. Used by permission.

college found much which he had believed, in the simple, pious home where he grew up, challenged. He felt he must almost abandon the Christian faith. He revealed his doubts to a friend, and had many a discussion with him. Then one day that friend said bluntly to him, "Horace, are you living up to the level of the truth you do see?"

It was a good question. Many make of intellectual questionings an escape from involvement. We live on the basis of our doubts rather than the positive beliefs of our minds. Sometimes the course we take is even less worthy of us; we use our doubts to cover our timidity and our fear, to avoid taking our place in the struggle.

If we are willing to set out on the road with him, we find the light grows in our mind. In the act of obedience and in the very struggle itself the flash of truth reaches us.

I wonder if there are any who do not have questionings about some clause of the Christian creed. Do we not all repeat some phrases of the historic creedal statements of the church as an act of faith rather than as an expression of full personal conviction?

I confess to adopting this course of action in relation to the clause in the Apostles' Creed: "I believe in the Holy Spirit." I accepted it, because the church declared it, but it held difficulties for me personally, and virtually was without meaning.

Then, one day, it all became alive for me. With glowing wonder I believed. The Holy Spirit was given for comfort, for guidance, for strength. He does convict of sin and of righteousness. Having journeyed on, almost in blind faith, at this point the light at last broke. I believed.

It is along the risky road with Jesus, rather than in detachment, that he is often able to reveal new truths to us. But first we must be ready to set out with him. "Let us also go, that we may die with him."

Many times in the story of Jesus abiding truth is expressed in the dialogue between Jesus and some questioner. The world owes a debt of gratitude to the men and women who probed beneath the surface and drew forth the answers Jesus had to give.

Thomas fulfilled this role in the Upper Room in Jerusalem on the night before the crucifixion. Jesus spoke in terms which were no doubt mysterious to all his hearers. He said he was going to leave them, but that later they would join him in a place which he would prepare for them. It was Thomas who was bold enough to express his confusion and to voice his doubts. "Lord, we do not know where you are going; how can we know the way?" He brought forth one of the greatest sentences Jesus ever spoke: "I am the way, and the truth, and the life."

A child learns by asking questions. In maturity knowledge increases by the same process. The pity is many of us cease to use it. We accept easily, uncritically what is told us. We miss the new revelations God had for us had we continued asking, asking.

There is a time in intellectual quest when we should pause and wait for new light to come. It is like fishing with a gut line. When it becomes tangled, perhaps in the darkness, knots are only tightened, tangles made worse when it is pulled or tugged at. The best course of action is to put it in a bowl of water. When it is taken out later the tangles almost fall out.

Some doubts, after we have asked all the questions we can in an effort to get an answer, should be put to one side. We wait for new experiences to come, new light to dawn. Then in time the answer may appear.

Religion, no less than science, owes much to those who go on asking questions when others are ready to accept the word of authority. It was Thomas, the honest questioner and doubter, who brought from the mind of Jesus the revelation that he regarded himself as "the way, and the truth, and the life."

After the resurrection of Jesus, Thomas, by doubting, makes his greatest contribution to the Christian story. Through him comes tremendous evidence of the convincing power of the fact of the resurrection.

Thomas was not present with the other disciples when Jesus first appeared to them. He was not prepared to accept so stupendous an event on secondhand testimony. He must see for himself. "Unless I see in his hands the print of the nails, and place my finger in the mark of the nails, and place my hand in his side, I will not believe."

One of the charges against the authenticity of the

132

resurrection is that Jesus only appeared to those who were predisposed to accept the miracle. It might have been, so it is said, a case of wish fulfillment. They saw what they wanted and expected to see.

No claim of this kind can be laid against Thomas. He did not expect to see a risen Christ, and when the testimony of others was heard he refused to accept it. He was frankly incredulous that a man should rise from the dead.

Thus it is tremendously impressive that Thomas, Thomas the doubter, came to believe that Jesus was alive. Doubt apparently led to full faith. Thomas felt the full impact of the convincing power of the resurrection.

Thomas, by being slow to believe, brought forth a further wonderful truth concerning the risen Christ. When Jesus at last confronted him he said: "Put your finger here, and see my hands; . . . and place it in my side."

There must have been a deep fear in the minds of the disciples that even if Jesus were risen from the dead, he would not be the same master and friend. If a beggar man became king, he could easily be so changed as to be no longer available to his former friends. In his risen state would Jesus be the same?

Thomas found the answer. Jesus showed him his hands and his side. He was the same. The last picture of Jesus which had burned itself on the disciples' minds was of the cross on Calvary. They could not forget those blood-red wounds in Jesus' hands and feet and side. His risen body revealed those same marks of suffering. There was clear continuity between the Jesus they had known and loved and the Christ in his resurrection glory.

Jesus, in the forty days between the resurrection and the ascension, was training, disciplining his men. He was preparing them to live without his visible presence, but he was also seeking to show them he was still at their side. The only difference in the future would be they would not be able to see him with their physical eyes. In every other respect he would be as they had known him in those three wonderful years along the roads of Palestine.

Thomas got the message. He realized that the risen Christ was the same as the historic Jesus. He grasped the companion truth, that because Christ was risen, he had always been more than just another teacher or prophet. So his faith, by many a tortuous route and through many a doubt, blazed into certainty. It was Thomas who gave voice to the most profound and exalted declaration of faith in all the New Testament. Before the risen Christ he bowed: "My Lord and my God!"

JESUS
AND THE MAN
WHO FAILED

Every one of us knows what it
is to live with a sense of failure. Sometimes it is defeat
within, when the seduction of temptation proves too
strong for us and we fall. Sometimes it is a failure in
personal relationships, with fumbling and bungling
creating bitterness, even hatred. Sometimes life itself
seems to have passed us by, and we become conscious of
failure in the race of life. Sometimes we know we have
failed on the deepest level of all, we have failed God.

There is a wonderful story in the Bible of how Jesus dealt with a man who failed. It is the story of Peter. With infinite wisdom and tenderness Jesus brought hope and recovery to one whose failure was so complete it could have been fatal.

Among the disciples of Jesus, Peter was always first. He was the first to be called. Peter and his brother Andrew had a fishing business in Capernaum when Jesus invited them to become "fishers of men." Leaving all, they followed him. In all the lists of disciples Peter's name appears first. Often he was the first to speak, assuming the position of leader in that small band of men. He was the first to call Jesus the Christ, winning the comment from his Master that on this faith would the church be built. He was first to proclaim the message of the resurrection of Jesus to the people of Jerusalem on the day of Pentecost. Peter was the first leader to be recognized by the church as it established itself in the ancient world.

It was Peter who, apart from Judas, failed more ignominiously than any other. When the enemies of Jesus came to arrest him in the Garden of Gethsemane the devastating comment appears: "They all forsook him and fled." Running with them was Peter, the man who had boasted he would fight, he would die for Jesus.

Then followed Peter's denial in the judgment hall that he ever knew Jesus. When asked if he were a companion of Jesus he said: "I do not know the man." At once an abject sense of failure overwhelmed him, and he went out into the night and wept bitter tears of shame and remorse.

For Peter there was a glorious sequel. When Jesus rose from the dead the message came that the risen Christ wanted to meet his men in Galilee. The message said: "Tell my disciples—and Peter."

We have the story fortunately of the meeting of Jesus and Peter in Galilee after the resurrection. Something happened there which set the feet of Peter on the road to recovery and restoration. With a renewal of trust Peter resumes his place of leadership. The man who was a failure goes on until in utter faithfulness he finally receives the martyr's crown.

How does Jesus stop failures from being fatal? How does he take hold of us when we have fallen, and put us once more on our feet? How does Jesus help people who have failed?

Nothing is clearer in the dealings of Jesus with people who failed than that he was always taking the initiative to bring about restoration. At the moment of deepest despondency he always brought hope.

The news that Jesus was alive and that he wanted to see the disciples in Galilee must have fallen with a thud of despair into Peter's heart. It could not have included him. He had so failed in the hour of testing that no place remained for him. In the face of Christ's warning he had fallen. Peter, by his words and actions, had excluded himself from the disciple band.

Then came the startling reversal. Mary brought the

message: "Go, tell his disciples and Peter that he is going before you to Galilee; there you will see him, as he told you." Peter heard these words with unbelievable joy. He was included! There was a special message just for him! "And Peter—and Peter!"

We have every right to infer this excitement on Peter's part because the report of these two words, "and Peter," appears only in Mark's Gospel. It is a widely accepted fact that Mark virtually reported in his Gospel Peter's memories, Peter's account of the life of Jesus. It was Peter who remembered those two words which were really a message of invitation: "And Peter."

I suppose it is always true that the man or the woman with the greatest resources of mind and emotion can both climb the heights of achievement and plumb the depths of defeat. The more timid and colorless people may not record great and spectacular failures, but they also do not reveal noble victories.

Anton Boison tells of meeting a man who had been with him in his university days and who had entered forestry service. This man was telling his experiences to a group of friends when one said: "Say, Bill, have you ever been lost?" With some heat the reply was given: "Lost? Of course I've been lost. It's only the dubs who never go five miles from camp who don't get lost sometimes."

Jesus knew the value of Peter. He was a man who was capable of anything. He may have boasted he

138

would never fail. He may have pressed on beyond the other disciples. Was it not Peter who first called Jesus the Christ? So he was capable of a great fall. But Jesus didn't allow him to stay defeated. Christ's hand, taking the initiative, reached out to lift him again to his feet.

How many of us could tell of this kind of experience? Pressed deep within our consciousness is the sense of failure. We imagine we could never rise again. But then, amid our shame and self-condemnation, a word of hope seems to reach us. We are stirred amid the black depression to fight back. Christ has spoken, and we take heart and courage.

Norman Vincent Peale, the New York minister, tells how Christ reached him with a message of hope amid failure. After two years at the Marble Collegiate Church in New York he could see only failure. While on vacation in England he faced the issue, suggesting to his wife that he should admit he had failed and resign.

Then, as many a man would have to admit, the voice of his wife became the voice of hope and courage: "You are a failure, but not in the way you think," she said bluntly.

You're a failure because you've let yourself be overwhelmed by the fear of failure. You are thinking entirely of yourself, and your success and popularity—or lack of it. You're not thinking about what God may have in mind for you. Maybe he wants you to despair so that you can help despairing people.

In any case, why don't you practice what you preach? Why don't you put your life in God's hands, surrender yourself to Jesus Christ and ask for his guidance?

Ask the Lord to help you get back to him. You've lost contact for a little while, that's all. Once you're back in touch these difficulties that seem so large will iron themselves out.

"You really think so?" Mr. Peale asked.

"I know so," she said. "Go on. Right now, right here and now."

"All right," he said, and reached for her hand. Then he bowed his head and closed his eyes and began to pray.

None of us needs ever surrender to failure. Christ never does. Amid our most abject defeats he stands, calling to us to fight back.

"And Peter." Perhaps we should put our own name in Peter's place. He speaks to you and me: "Go tell my disciples—and Jean, Mary, Albert, John—I will meet you in Galilee."

Jesus helped Peter by forcing him to face the memory of his failure, and by facing it, to deal with it.

There are two ways of handling moral failure. One is to minimize it, to bring relief to the conscience by insisting that the offense is not as serious in God's sight as we may imagine. There are times when this is the treatment needed to ease the burden of guilt.

On the other hand, sometimes it is right to lift the threshold of conscience, to increase distress by emphasizing the seriousness of the inner collapse or the outer betrayal. Then by receiving God's forgiveness the laboring conscience can find peace.

A wonderful picture is given in Galilee of how Jesus brought love to bear on the failure of Peter. He did it by forcing Peter to face the memory of what he had done, and by facing it to destroy once and for all its power to fester and poison.

Far from overlooking or minimizing Peter's denial, Jesus recalls it to mind. He does it in a number of ways.

A charcoal fire is burning by the sea of Galilee when the disciples come ashore to meet the risen Christ. There is only one other place in the New Testament where a charcoal fire is mentioned. It is in the judgment hall where Peter, while he warmed himself, three times denied his Lord.

Three times the question comes to Peter: "Do you love me?" Three times the cock crowed when Peter failed. The significance of the thrice-repeated question would hardly have been lost on Peter. We can almost see his wince of pain.

"Simon, son of John . . . ?" Jesus had given Simon a new name, Peter. Now he is using the old name, taking him back to the point where Simon had chosen a new life.

"Follow me." These simple words were the exact words addressed to Peter three years before as he had left his all to become a disciple of Jesus. With subtlety Jesus is telling Peter he must begin again and that he

141

can begin again. He is being challenged afresh to take the road with Jesus, now the risen Christ.

Galilee is the place where it is all happening, and Galilee was the place of beginnings. There, by the lakeside, there amid the fisherfolk, the nets, and the ships, all was being reenacted. Jesus was offering Peter the chance of starting all over again.

With what infinite tenderness, with what divine surgery of soul Jesus seeks the restoration, the healing of Peter. Peter's denial had been a traumatic experience. Not easily could the wound be healed.

Jesus seeks healing by bringing all out into the open. He forces Peter to look at what had happened in his presence. Then, facing it together, it could be forgiven and forgotten.

When we fail, how often we try to hide from ourselves the truth. We call our collapse by some less serious name, as though that changes its nature. We highlight some mitigating circumstances, hoping that a mumbled alibi will ease the pain. Like Adam of old we blame someone else, as though the fact that we were tempted provides some excuse. We point to someone else's failure, suggesting almost that the failure of many somehow minimizes our own.

Jesus allows no escape. He calls on us to face our failures. Gently he brings all to the surface. He wants no inner festering which can retard recovery. He wants a clean wound for healing. So, deeply he probes. Then, having laid bare the need he applies the salve of forgiveness, the deep full forgiveness of God.

> I know not how that Calvary's Cross
> A world from sin could free:
> I only know its matchless love
> Has brought God's love to me.

Nothing is more moving in Christ's treatment of Peter than the way he shows he trusts him still. By giving Peter a task to do he opens the way to recovery.

When Peter, the leader of the disciple band, failed, he must have thought he would never be trusted again. With what eagerness he must have heard the words: "Feed my lambs, . . . tend my sheep, . . . feed my sheep."

On the surface it may appear Peter is being given the same charge three times. There are differences. Peter is trusted with the care of children and those who would be beginners in the Christian way: "Feed my lambs." The second command is: "Tend my sheep." He is called to exercise general oversight of the adult followers of Christ. "Feed my sheep" is the third commission. Peter is to supply the needs of the mature members of Christ's flock.

One fact, and one fact alone, must have throbbed in Peter's mind. He was still trusted by Christ. There was a place reserved for him in the kingdom's service.

The history of the Christian church is full of stories of God taking hold of men and women who were failures and even using failure as an equipment for fuller service. God it seems is able to use even sin for his glory.

From the early days of the Methodist Church in Australia comes a story of what God can do. The first circuit steward—principal official in a Methodist church—was a man named Edward Eager.

Edward Eager was a forger. Educated for the bar in Ireland, he was convicted of forgery and sentenced to transportation as a convict to Australia.

Before leaving his Irish prison Edward Eager was soundly converted through the visit of a Methodist preacher. On reaching Australia he became one of the founders of the Methodist Church. His exemplary conduct won for him release, and he became a highly respected member of the colony. He recommenced his professional career, becoming a well-known figure at the courts.

When the first Methodist circuit was organized, Edgar Eager was elected as circuit steward. As he grew in wealth and influence he greatly served the growing church. It was Edward Eager who gave £1,000 toward the erection of the second Methodist Church in Macquarie Street, Sydney. Later he was responsible for a well-thought-out plan for the establishment of a mission to the Australian Aborigines.

The last we hear of Edward Eager is when, in 1821, he was elected by the colonists as delegate to present a legal case before the state authorities in London. And so the man who had left his native land as a convict returned in honor, a living tribute to what Christ can do with failure when a life is placed in his hands.

When do we trust again someone who has failed? This is a question the church has often been forced to ask. A member, a lay leader, a minister falls into sin. The name of the church must be protected. Evil must not seem to be condoned. A disciplined membership is necessary. Yet beyond these questions are even deeper issues. How shall a fallen man be helped to his feet? How shall divine grace be set flowing again?

Jesus never looks upon moral failures as fatal. After Peter's deep and bitter defeat Jesus again showed his trust. And how wonderfully his trust was justified, for not again did this man fail. In the story of the early church one man stands out, his record justifying the name given him: Peter, rocklike! And Jesus said: "Feed my sheep."

Jesus wins from Peter a new act of dedication. Through it Christ was able steadily to fashion a man fit to lead the early church, and an example for all time.

I find it full of meaning that Jesus issued the same challenge to Peter in Galilee at the beginning and the end of his earthly ministry. "Follow me," he said. Each time Peter gave the response of faith and obedience.

Yet was that response the same? When as a fisherman Peter set out to follow Jesus he could have known little about him. At the end it was different. He had lived through the three years of Christ's ministry. He had faced the tumultuous experiences of the trial,

145

death, and resurrection. Now he knew that at the heart
of discipleship was a cross. Indeed, there was an
ominous warning of suffering to come in the prophecy: "You will stretch out your hands, and another will
gird you and carry you where you do not wish to go."
There falls across these words not Christ's but Peter's
cross—the cross on which he was to die a martyr's
death.

In other words, Peter's second response was a far
more calculated and deliberate act. Now something of
the price of being a follower of Jesus was clear. Yet
he did not flinch. Now Peter offered a new and deeper
dedication.

If tradition can be believed, Christ's prophecy came
true. The day came when Peter and his wife were led
out to be crucified. With that streak of cruelty which
appears to be part of human nature in the ascendancy,
Peter's wife was crucified first, and he was forced to
watch her die. With the quiet words, "Remember the
Lord," he encouraged her until the agony ceased.

Then it was Peter's turn to "stretch forth his hands."
Believing he was not worthy to die as had his Lord,
Peter requested that he be crucified upside down. So
Peter follows his Master, this time to the end, and fail-
ure was perfected in obedience.

During the last years of his life the artist Herbert
Beecroft lived in Sydney. I visited him often and heard
him tell how his famous "Head of Christ" came to be
painted.

Herbert Beecroft was one day reading the story of the trial of Jesus. He came to the denial of Jesus by Peter where it says that Jesus looked at Peter: "And Peter remembered and went and wept bitterly."

The artist moved into his small garden, meditating on those words: "And Peter remembered." Suddenly he saw as though projected before his eyes the face of Christ in that moment in the judgment hall. Rushing inside he sketched rapidly the outline of the features, the expression of face which he had seen in Jesus. Within a few days the painting was finished. The world had been given Beecroft's "Head of Christ."

Jesus knows how to deal with people who have failed. Just as well, for who among us does not need him? Beyond our failure comes his call: "Follow me." He is literally once again asking us to take the road with him. He is trying to convince us that all may answer his summons, even people like you and me who are failures.

JESUS
AND A MAN WITH
SPIRITUAL DESIRES

Some time ago my wife and I sat perched on an observation platform in a game reserve in Central Africa. It was the end of the dry season, and the land was brown and parched. We were told that if we waited long enough we would see most species of animals, for they would all come, driven by thirst to drink water at the pool.

It was a fascinating experience there in the early

morning. Across the pool was a pride of nine lions, and of course nothing appeared until they came and went. Then began the strangest procession I have ever seen. Slowly there came to drink a herd of deer. They were followed by a colony of baboons. Warthogs, zebras, and a small herd of buffalo came to slake their thirst. Not far away were the tall giraffes and the lumbering elephants, awaiting their turns.

Everything comes to water, so the tourist publicity had claimed. And everything did. As I thought of it all there came to mind the sentence from the Bible:

> As the hart longs
>   for flowing streams,
> so longs my soul
>   for thee, O God.

There is a story in the life of Jesus where we meet a man who was driven by deep spiritual desires, as an animal is driven to seek for water. In it we see how Jesus helps people who seek for God.

There came one day to Jesus one who was called the rich young ruler. I think this is a misnomer. He apparently was rich, but he was not exactly young. When Jesus mentioned the commandments he replied, "All these have I kept from my youth up" (KJV). Only someone who had moved beyond youth would surely speak in such terms.

I suggest the so-called "rich young ruler" was a well-to-do, successful man already in the younger mid-years of life. Perhaps having found comfort and success, he realized how limited was the satisfaction they brought. Like many before and since he sought deeper answers to the mystery of life. To Jesus he comes seeking those answers: "Good Master, what good thing must I do, that I may have eternal life?" (KJV).

The reply Jesus gives must have seemed trite and disappointing: "Keep the commandments." His face falls. He has heard all that before. Then Jesus goes deeper. "Go, sell what you possess and give to the poor." Give up all he possessed! He could not take it. The answer is starkly different from what he expected. Slowly he pushes through the crowd. Now his back rather than his face is toward Jesus. We watch him, shoulders humped, as he walks away, until he is swallowed up in the milling people and is gone.

There throbs in every life a great and compelling thirst, the thirst for God. As Aldous Huxley has said: "There is a God-shaped blank in modern man's heart." It is an emptiness only the shape of God can fill.

A feature of our time is the spiritual wistfulness of millions of people. In the older areas of Christendom where so often faith has died, the yearning for God has not been silenced.

In the city of Sydney there has commenced a "Dial-a-Prayer" service. By dialing a certain telephone number it is possible at any time of day or night to hear a short prayer, recorded electronically. Every week the prayer is changed.

150

The amazing fact is the immense number of people who call for that prayer. The peak period is during the day, when from business houses, offices, and homes under the pressure of living the mute cry for spiritual help rises. In the first year of operation no less than 327,000 called "Dial-a-Prayer."

At least in Australia it is easier to preach the gospel of Jesus today than at any time in my ministry. Masses of the people are not found in any church, but they are ready to listen on wharves, in factories, and at universities to the Christian message. It provides further evidence of the hunger and thirst for God which are part of our society.

It is time perhaps that we remember what may be called Christian anthropology. Such an interpretation of human nature begins with the arresting statements of the first book of the Bible. God says there: "Let us make man in our image." So it was: "God breathed; . . . and man became a living being."

Elsewhere the Bible bears witness to man's hunger after God. In the book of Ecclesiastes appears the sentence: "He has put eternity into man's mind." "Deep calls unto deep," says the book of Psalms. Jesus himself bears witness to that thirst when he cries: "If any one thirst, let him come to me and drink," and, "Whoever drinks of the water that I shall give him will never thirst."

Sooner or later we all stand beside the attractive, successful man who came to Jesus. For a time we might

151

silence the deeper desires of our hearts, but they will not be denied forever.

It may be some great disappointment which forces us to reassess the meaning of life and the basis of true human satisfaction. It may be when we watch someone we love slipping beyond our reach that we face the facts of life and death. It may be the sudden realization that we are not as young as we used to be which sets us counting up the worth of the way we have chosen. It may be under the spell of some intense silence or the inspiration of great music or drama or the experience of worship that we hear unmistakably the cry of our own soul.

William Blake knew of such moments of intense spiritual desire. With one of his poems he has an appealing illustration. It shows a little man with strangely large hands and arms standing at the foot of a ladder. The ladder pushes so far up into the clouds that its top is lost to view.

The little man, looking up, is just saying: "I want, I want." That is as far as he goes. He wants, but he does not know what he wants.

This is where so many of us stand. We who are made in the image of God cannot forever be satisfied with anything, anyone less than God. In the end not only animals must come to water to drink, man must find and drink of the water of life.

Spiritual desire must flow out into social responsibility. This is the firm message the man received who came to Jesus seeking eternal life.

A somewhat strange direction is taken in the conversation in the New Testament. "Good Master," is the form of address. But Jesus objects to being called "good." He is not interested in words of adulation and flattery. He knows these can be a way of escape from facing reality.

Then it is that the challenge to keep the commandments is given. Some of the commandments are named: "You shall not steal. You shall not kill. You shall not bear false witness. Honor your father and your mother." Those named are what may be called the social commandments. They are the ones which govern human relationships and social obligations.

Next Christ's questioner is forced to examine what he is doing with his wealth. The suggestion is that he is using it to serve his own self-interests. He is told to go and sell what he has and give all to the poor. Again spiritual desire is to express itself in social responsibility.

There is great danger, it seems to me, in much modern popular religion. The semireligious popular tune which reaches the radio "hit parade" reveals spiritual interests, but little else. Christmas carols and candlelight services are pretty, but can represent cheap religion. The Hollywood spectacular religious film falls into the same category. All underline the fact of a widespread interest in religion, but of itself this interest can become a parody of religion.

John Baillie in his Gifford Lectures *A Sense of the Presence of God* emphasizes with great power that there is only one way by which we can show our love of God—it is by loving our neighbor. He says: "The purpose of divine love is not that we should return love to God: . . . it is that he who is called should serve his neighbour in love."

Is this where the church has often gone astray? I think of the "all night hymn sings" in Tennessee. I think of the endless ritualistic services of the church where language is strained to express adulation of God. I think of the millions who stream to churches on Sunday often appearing to make the worship, the adoration of God, an end in itself.

I remember vividly being one of a deputation of four Methodist ministers who went to see the prime minister of Australia in an effort to settle the great postwar coal strike. We were shown into the office of the late J. B. Chifley, then prime minister.

Mr. Chifley had just returned from abroad. Before we talked about the coal miners, he spoke of some of his overseas impressions. He had visited Rome, and as a practicing Roman Catholic had been given an audience with the pope. That same night he asked to be shown the city, especially the poorer areas of Rome. With bitter words he condemned what he saw, the hovels of the poor, the degradation he had discovered within the very shadow of mighty St. Peter's Cathedral and the pomp and splendor of the Vatican.

Does all this come under condemnation in the words of Jesus: Do not call me "good"—keep the commandments? Certainly one who knew the mind of Jesus intimately makes this point. John says: "If a man says, 'I love God,' and hates his brother, he is a liar, for he who does not love his brother whom he has seen, cannot love God whom he has not seen." Spiritual desire must, yes it must, flow out in social obligation.

We see Jesus, by every means at his disposal, trying to lead the man before him to the fulfillment of his desires. But the challenge is too much, and we see him turning away and pushing through the crowds. There is a note of infinite pathos in the story, for "Jesus looking upon him loved him."

I have a picture in my study which catches the moment of challenge and possibility. It shows Jesus with his hand on the shoulder of the man who had come to him. His other hand is pointing away into the distance, directing toward the thrilling road ahead. There are uncertainty, confusion, trouble in the face of the one called to discipleship. He appears near to the moment of decision. It is the wrong decision, and he goes away sorrowful.

Life is very attractive today where I live, in pleasant sunny Australia. Prosperity is high, and freedom and opportunity are expansive. None would deny the attractiveness, the thrill of living for so many!

A new craze is sweeping through our young people. It is the craze of surfboard riding. For many a young Australian to be able to ride a mountainous wave without suffering a "wipe out" is life at its thrilling best. As one young surfboard rider put it: "It is more exciting than sex."

In that comment is expressed the real alternative in Australia today to the life Christ offers. The thrills which satisfactions of the flesh give seem to be the apex of living. Sensual satisfaction, the excitement of the sporting contest, the joy of speed and risk in the clean, crisp water of an Australian surf represent life at its thrilling best.

Yet the words of William Temple stand: "The great individual is the man who is reacting to the greatest number of the elements in Reality, the greatest variety of its aspects." He who responds only to stimulus on the physical level of existence is but partially alive.

I wonder if you know that moving incident in Boris Pasternak's novel *Dr. Zhivago* where a young man faces execution. His name is Terrenty Galuzin. With a number of others he is taken to the edge of a cliff and lined up to be shot.

Suddenly his nerve breaks. He grovels before his captors, pleading with them: "Forgive me, comrades, I'm sorry, I won't do it again, please let me off. Don't kill me. I haven't lived yet."

I could not get that last pathetic sentence out of my mind for days: "I haven't lived yet." This is the cry which should be on the lips of every man, every woman who has not yet accepted Jesus Christ and his way of life.

Think of what the man whose spiritual desires had brought him to Jesus was losing as he hurried away through the crowd, turning his back on the vision glorious that had come to him.

He was missing a great adventure, the great adventure of serving Jesus Christ. He could have stepped out on the road with Jesus, stepped into history. But he missed it for the sake of a few miserable possessions.

He was missing a great friendship. Christ there on the roadside was offering his companionship. He was turning his back on the friendship of Jesus Christ.

He was missing a great development. We know what companionship with Jesus did for Peter and James and John. They grew in stature as the years passed. None could prophesy what this man with all his attractiveness and advantages would have become.

He was missing a great satisfaction. There is no life on earth to equal fighting the devil and living in obedience to God. When spiritual desires are satisfied we have found the secret of complete fulfillment of life.

To obtain this life Christ offers is worth the selling and sacrificing of everything. And this is precisely what is demanded. "Go, sell all, . . . and follow me." It is all or nothing. Spiritual desire must flow out in obedience to God or it remains useless. To live for Christ's sake is to live fully.

How Jesus Helped People

The adequacy of Christ is expressed in the hymn which was written by a young schoolteacher for the 1963 Mission to South Africa. With deep faith and simple language it points to the answer every one of us may find as spiritual desires stir within us.

> Christ enough to break all barriers;
> Christ enough in peace, in strife;
> Christ enough to build our nation;
> Christ enough for death, for life.
> Christ enough for old and lonely;
> Christ enough for those who fall;
> Christ enough to save the sin-sick;
> Christ enough for one—for all! [1]

[1] John Gardener, "Mission Hymn." Used by permission.